SHELTERING IN THE BACKRUSH
A HISTORY OF TWIN ISLANDS

SHELTERING *in the* BACKRUSH

A History of Twin Islands

Jeanette Taylor

HARBOUR PUBLISHING

Copyright © 2023 Jeanette Taylor

1 2 3 4 5 — 27 26 25 24 23

All rights reserved. No part of this publication may be reproduced, stored in a retrieval system or transmitted, in any form or by any means, without prior permission of the publisher or, in the case of photocopying or other reprographic copying, a licence from Access Copyright, www.accesscopyright.ca, 1-800-893-5777, info@accesscopyright.ca.

Harbour Publishing Co. Ltd.
P.O. Box 219, Madeira Park, BC, V0N 2H0
www.harbourpublishing.com

Edited by Ariel Brewster
Cover design by Dwayne Dobson
Text design by Carleton Wilson
Printed and bound in Canada

 Canada Council for the Arts / Conseil des Arts du Canada

 BRITISH COLUMBIA ARTS COUNCIL |  BRITISH COLUMBIA
Supported by the Province of British Columbia

Harbour Publishing acknowledges the support of the Canada Council for the Arts, the Government of Canada, and the Province of British Columbia through the BC Arts Council.

Library and Archives Canada Cataloguing in Publication

Title: Sheltering in the backrush : a history of Twin Islands / Jeanette Taylor.
Other titles: History of Twin Islands
Names: Taylor, Jeanette, 1953- author.
Description: Includes bibliographical references and index.
Identifiers: Canadiana (print) 20220497648 | Canadiana (ebook) 20220497818 | ISBN 9781990776113 (softcover) | ISBN 9781990776120 (EPUB)
Subjects: LCSH: British Columbia—History.
Classification: LCC FC3845.T92 T39 2023 | DDC 971.1/204—dc23
ISBN 978-1-990776-11-3 (paper)
ISBN 978-1-990776-12-0 (ebook)

Sheltering in the Backrush: A History of Twin Islands, is dedicated to Mark Torrance, whose vision and enthusiasm made this book a reality.

Prologue 9

Chapter One: In the Beginning 13

Chapter Two: Tied Together 17

Chapter Three: A Homesteader's Lot 28

Chapter Four: Asian Roots 44

Chapter Five: Twin Islands Lodge 62

Chapter Six: Living the Dream 83

Chapter Seven: Turbulence 97

Chapter Eight: Fit for a Queen 110

Chapter Nine: The White Knight 122

Chapter Ten: Contemplating Eternity 132

Chapter Eleven: Serendipity 139

Chapter Twelve: Taking Wing 145

Acknowledgements 152

Index 154

Bibliography 157

About the Author 159

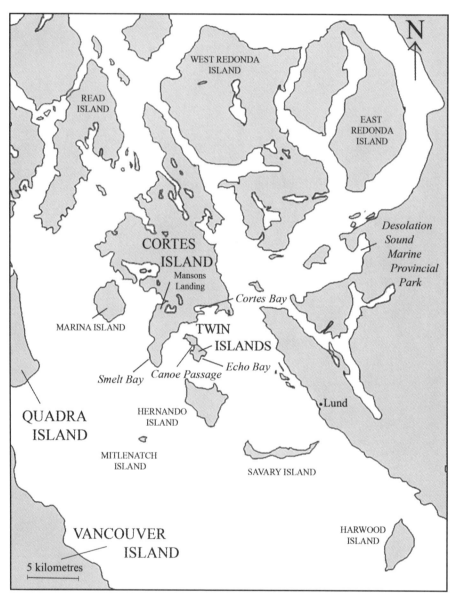

Map of Twin Islands and surrounding area.

PROLOGUE

Sheltering in the Backrush: A History of Twin Islands, Jeanette Taylor, Dec 5, 2022

Twin Islands, a private retreat just off the entrance to Desolation Sound Marine Park, is a small place with a big story. I wrote cameo sketches of some of the islands' live-wire characters in *Tidal Passages*, a book about the Discovery Islands. They run the gamut, from the ancestors of the Tla'amin people to German and British royalty, an Irish aristocrat (whose murder remains a mystery), spies and espionage, newspaper moguls, movie stars and a visionary heiress.

Tidal Passages led me to Mark Torrance, the current owner of Twin Islands. Descendants of the Andrews family had sent him a large collection of World War II-era photographs documenting the construction of a massive log lodge, which remains largely as built in the late 1930s. Among them were sepia-toned images of people: digging clams on a beach, tending livestock, celebrating Christmas and posing with fish. Mark wanted to know these people's stories—and, indeed, all the stories from Twin Islands' past—so we joined forces.

The Andrews family's photos became our starting point. In one of them, two young men gaze directly into the camera, their faces lit with amusement. They're dressed in working garb, one in a flat, wide-brimmed cap and the other in a heavily creased jacket. Two of the women with them have their hands clasped in an awkward pose, as if caught off-guard. One wears a knee-length coat with a stylish plaid collar and cuffs, while a woman nearby seems impervious to the cold, in her thin housedress and an open bomber jacket.

In sharp contrast to this group—who I was to learn were members of the crew who built Twin Islands Lodge—are three women in heavy leopard skin, sable and mink coats. The one with a hat with a curled brim is Ethel Andrews, the matriarch of her family. She and her husband, Dick, had recently bought Twin Islands as a getaway from a world on the cusp of war.

Everyone in the picture is smiling, or appears faintly amused. It's a happy occasion; perhaps a first chance for the Andrews family to see the lodge as it neared completion. The crew would have ensured the fir floors were polished and gleaming in the shadowy light of the log walls.

I tracked down the descendants of both the Andrews family and their crew and uploaded their respective photos onto cloud storage. They were moved by what they saw.

"I must say, I had a strong emotional reaction, weeping; and, as I write this, I start again," wrote Rita Rasmussen, the daughter of construction foreman Charlie Rasmussen. There were pictures she'd never seen before of her parents in their youthful prime and her elder brother as a child. Rita had to run through the Andrews family's photos three times before she could show them to her husband with only "minor snivelling." She had grown up on stories of Twin Islands Lodge, which was her father's proudest achievement.

John Harrison, an Andrews descendant, had a similar reaction as he clicked through the Rasmussen's photos, finding images of his grandparents and his mother as a sparky young woman. There were tears on his side of the screen too.

As we chronicled successive decades, repeating themes emerged. From the poorest to the richest, Twin Islanders love to cook, drawing upon the bounty of the land and sea. They're dog people through and through, and keen birders. They're deeply moved by nature. And all of them have lived exceptional lives, impacted by global events.

They're a family of sorts, having fallen under what Mark Torrance describes as 'Twin's spell.' "So far, all the owners have, with no guiding vision, built upon each other's efforts to create a legacy," he wrote in reflections upon Twin Islands.

Mark spent over two decades updating the islands' buildings and infrastructure. "Our work mirrored the Andrews family's initial concept for

PROLOGUE

Tonie Wong, Marian Andrews and Ethel Andrews with a few members of their construction crew, who were building a massive log lodge on Twin Islands in the late 1930s. With the Andrews family are Charlie Rasmussen, construction foreman (centre back), and his wife Helge, the cook for the crew. The three people with them (right) are unknown. *Marian (Andrews) Harrison collection, courtesy John Harrison*

the lodge," he wrote, "introducing cutting-edge technology. They installed radiophones, flush toilets and electricity, and we brought the internet to the region and clean energy to Twin. Today, on Twin, our creature comforts are supplied by solar and hydro power harnessed from the earth and sun, and we draw our inner power from immersion in the natural world."

I too fell under Twin's spell: kayaking its rocky shores, crunching through the litter of an arbutus forest and camped beneath Douglas firs, with an eagle swooping close overhead to warn me away from its nest.

The beauty of the islands is captivating, but it's her people who have taken root in my imagination—as they will yours.

On one of my first visits, during initial research, I lay in the tall, yellowing grass of the homestead meadow in Canoe Passage, where the Tla'amin people once had seasonal camps. Above the slap of the waves and the distant screech of eagles and ravens, there were whispers of past lives. There were ghosts in that meadow. Many ghosts. Ghosts with stories to tell.

And I was on a quest to tease out those stories.

CHAPTER ONE

In the Beginning

An aerial view c. 1938 of Twin Islands, looking east to the mainland. *Andrews Coll, courtesy of John Harrison*

Twin Islands forms part of the lacy fringe at the southern edge of the Discovery Islands archipelago, where it meets the north Salish Sea. This is the interface between wilderness and urban settlement. To the north, heavily treed slopes rise vertically from the sea and fast tides churn through the constricted passages of a maze of islands and inlets. Navigating beyond this point is a white-knuckle challenge many recreational boaters avoid, ending

CHAPTER ONE

their travels to the east of Twin Islands in Desolation Sound Marine Park. To the south, the topography relaxes into a more habitable environment of open waters, benchlands, villages, towns and highways.

"Twin," as this pair of islands is known locally, is joined at low tide. Together, they comprise 281 hectares (694 acres) and are about 25 kilometres (16 miles) long. Twin hugs the southeast shore of Cortes Island, which has a year-round population of about 1,000 people. To the south is Hernando Island, an 890-hectare (2,200-acre) shared recreational property. Further south is Savary Island, which has roughly the same land mass as Twin and about 1,700 summer cottages vying for position along its sandy beaches.[1] In mid-channel is Mitlenatch Island, a bird sanctuary.

Stores and ferry services are available on Cortes, and across the channel at Lund there is a village founded by Scandinavian immigrants over a century ago. South of Lund is Teeshohsum, the home village of the Tla'amin people, who have lived on this part of the coast for thousands of years. Further south yet is the town of Powell River, facing Harwood and Texada Islands. On Twin's western horizon is Quadra Island, the largest of the Discovery Islands archipelago, and the town of Campbell River, backed by the ragged peaks of the Vancouver Island Ranges.

Twin lies within a geographical point of change. Two flood tides meet here, one curling upward from the south end of Vancouver Island, and the other squeezing down from the north through myriad passages. Twin and south Cortes straddle two climate zones, benefiting from a rain shadow effect, with heavier rainfall on the mountains to the east and west. While nearby Hernando sits squarely within the warmer Coastal Douglas-fir zone, north Cortes is characterized by the Coastal Western Hemlock zone.[2] Twin shares bits of both. Its lodgepole pines, found at higher elevations, give way to stands of heat-loving plants like arbutus trees and twisty manzanita

---

1 qathet Regional District, Planning Department.

2 Pottinger Gaherty Environmental Consultants, *Ecological Assessment of Twin Islands* (undertaken for Endswell in 1998), courtesy George Reifel. The assessment places Twin within two climate zones: CDFmm (Coastal Douglas-fir) and CWHxm1 (Coastal Western Hemlock). The islands do not have Garry oaks, but otherwise have plants found in both zones.

IN THE BEGINNING

Swirling bands of limestone at Iron Point on southeast Twin date back to the Upper Triassic period, over 2 million years ago. *Jeanette Taylor*

shrubs, both of which are at their northern limits.

Twin's geology is yet another of its distinctive features. Bands of compressed limestone on its southeast shore look like petrified waves breaking against blocky walls of cinnamon-coloured stone. In other places, the rocky shores look like bubbling black lava frozen into place to form hobbit-sized shelves, nooks, and crannies. According to local geologist David Caulfield, these outcrops burst to the surface in the Upper Triassic period over 200,000,000 years ago.[3]

The limestone bands found on Twin occur in just a handful of other places in the Discovery Islands, including Hernando. Marine fossils are embedded in the rock, which was compacted under tremendous pressure 90,000,000 years ago when two land masses collided, leaving a scar-like cleft that became the Salish Sea basin. "These processes are like a creeping conveyor belt that moved land masses at an almost indiscernible ten centimetres

---

3   David Caulfield, Masters of Science, P.Geo.

per year," says Caulfield, "but the magnitude of [the] force exerted broke, twisted, and folded the ductile limestone beds like toothpaste." The events and eras Caulfield describes defy the imagination, but the evidence is writ large on Twin's shores.

And then came the glaciers, engulfing all but the highest of British Columbia's mountain peaks about 30,000 years ago.[4] This was followed by warming periods, when melting glaciers scraped along the bedrock of the Salish Sea, depositing rocks, sand and rubble in their wake. Erratic boulders on Mitlenatch came from Toba Inlet, 63 kilometres (39 miles) to the northeast. The glaciers carved out a deep hollow in the centre of south Twin, depositing sediments that became a thick groundwater sponge for a large marsh.

As the burden of the melting glaciers eased about 12,000 years ago, land masses within the north Salish Sea rebounded, slowly rising to form the Discovery Islands, surrounded by a frigid ocean littered with ice flows. The higher elevations were the first to emerge and they were soon populated by birds, plants, animals—and humans.

---

4   Beamish and McFarlane, *The Sea Among Us: The Amazing Strait of Georgia* (Madeira Park: Harbour Publishing, 2014).

CHAPTER TWO

Tied Together

A young Indigenous man named Tl'umnachm is said to have carved this petroglyph of a whale on a large boulder to the south of Mansons Landing, on Cortes Island, after he gained spirit power during prolonged fasting and cleansing at Hague Lake. *Jeanette Taylor*

People laughed, ate, slept and loved on Twin Islands for thousands of years before the arrival of Europeans in the late 18th century, but we know nothing about them as individuals. Clues to their existence can be found in layered bands of shells, bones and fire-cracked rocks in three former seasonal

CHAPTER TWO

camps[5] in Canoe Passage, in fragmentary oral histories, and in the islands' place name: Tho'kwet, "to be tied together."[6] What emerges is a keyhole glance into a way of living that required a complex knowledge of tides, winds, seasons, and the movement of fish, birds and animals.

Twin lies within Tla'amin territory, which stretches from south Cortes to below present-day Powell River.[7] Together with the Klahoose of Toba Inlet, and the Xwemalhkwu[8] of Bute Inlet, the three groups are sometimes known collectively as the North Coast Salish. They share linguistic ties with people living as far south as Washington State. Their northern frontier is defined by the moat-like barrier of whirlpools and rapids off the mouth of Bute Inlet, beyond which live the Kwakwaka'wakw people, who have an entirely different language and customs.

Indigenous people have lived on the Discovery Islands since just after the retreat of the glaciers. Sites dating back more than 11,000 years have been recently found to the west of Twin, on the higher elevations of Quadra Island.[9] Scientists believe the First People travelled to this part of the coast from Asia in small boats, crossing a then-much-smaller Pacific Ocean.

The oldest known site in the immediate vicinity of Twin is Kahkaykay, "camping place," about 16 kilometres (10 miles) to the east in Grace Harbour, an inner branch of Okeover Arm. Extended families had permanent post and beam houses in this winter village, which was a congregation point for various North Coast Salish clans. Archaeology dates Kahkaykay

---

5   The provincial Archaeology Branch registered three sites on Twin in 1977: EaSf-29, EaSf-30 and EaSf-31.

6   Drew Blaney (Kespahl), Culture & Heritage Manager for the Tla'amin Nation, referring to the Band's *Traditional Use Study*.

7   Land claims are still in process, but Twin Islands is generally understood to lie within Tla'amin territory. See Dorothy Kennedy and Randy Bouchard, *Sliammon Life, Sliammon Lands*; and Homer G. Barnett, *The Coast Salish of British Columbia*, p. 29.

8   Formerly spelled Homalco.

9   Daryl Fedje, Duncan McLaren, Thomas S. James, Quentin Mackie, Nicole F. Smith, John R. Southon, Alexander P. Mackie, "A revised sea level history for the north Strait of Georgia, British Columbia, Canada," *Quaternary Science Reviews* 192(July 15, 2018):300–316, doi.org/10.1016/j.quascirev.2018.05.018.

back 7,000 years.[10]

The Tla'amin people moved with the seasons throughout their territory, depending upon the availability of fish, plants and animals. They maintained hundreds of seasonal sites, suggesting a population in the thousands before the ravages of European disease depopulated this coast.

An 1891 census noted that a man Europeans called Chief Tom,[11] his wife, Sophie, and two grown sons and their wives were camped in the Twin area. Exact locations weren't noted, but since their names follow that of an immigrant settler living in the Twin area, it's likely they were either camped in Echo Bay (on south Twin), Cortes Bay, or on nearby Hernando.

Chief Tom was born in about 1816, and Sophie was born some seven years later.[12] As an old man, the chief would describe cultural practices dating back to his grandparents' generation, before contact with Europeans. The right to use food-gathering sites like Twin was passed on from one generation to the next. The people of Twin likely wintered at Kw'uumaxen, "shelter inside arm," on southwest Cortes, now called Smelt Bay.[13] An archaeologist mapped the footprint of eleven communal houses in Smelt Bay Provincial Park.[14] But the village of Kw'uumaxen was once at least triple this size, stretching north along benchland for another 250 metres (820 feet) beyond park boundaries. Like most villages of this time, the houses stood in

---

10   Sarah Elizabeth Johnson, *A Tla'amin Cultural Landscape: Combining traditional knowledge with archaeological investigation in Grace Harbour, Desolation Sound, BC* (Burnaby: Simon Fraser University, MA thesis, 2010). A report for an archaeological dig on Texada Island, however, gives the date 7,500 BP. See Colleen Parsley, *Archaeological Impact Assessment of DjSc-1, Shelter Point Project* (Nanaimo: Aquilla Archaeology, 2013).

11   The census-taker spelled this man's name as Toma. However, Evan Adams, who is tracking Tla'amin families through Ancestry.ca, suggests this was Chief Tom, a Tla'amin elder who was an informant for anthropologist Homer Barnett in the 1930s.

12   These were the estimated birth years given in the 1891 census.

13   Homer Barnett, *The Coast Salish of British Columbia* (Eugene: University of Oregon Monographs, Studies in Anthropology, No. 4, September 1955).

14   William O. Angelbeck, *They Recognize No Superior Chief: Power, Practice, Anarchism and Warfare in the Coast Salish Past* (Vancouver: University of British Columbia, PhD thesis, April 2009), p. 252.

CHAPTER TWO

In spring the Tla'amin people divided into clan groups to go to seasonal food gathering sites like Twin Islands. Shell-packed earth marks places where they erected shelters like this one photographed by Edward Curtis in 1912. *Library of Congress*

a tight-packed row, facing into the winter sun above a sloped cobble beach. Elders must have sat on plank settees outside these houses, watching over children at play, their bright voices mingling with the calls of eagles, ravens and gulls while their parents filleted salmon and shelled clams.

In February, when herring returned to the area, chased by sea lions and salmon, it was a signal for kin groups to set off for their food-gathering camps. House boards were straddled across paired canoes to create platforms for children, boxes of fishing gear, clothing and tools. The Indigenous people would have drifted into the passage separating Twin on an incoming tide. Those of higher rank lashed their house boards onto shed-style frames they had left on-site, while slaves and people of lesser status erected simple lean-to tents draped with bulrush mats.

Rigorous work lay ahead. Women wove clams onto tri-pronged stakes they jabbed into the ground before the glowing coals of hot fires. Dried in this way, clams lasted for many months. Men loaded canoes with fishing spears, lines, weights and hooks to catch salmon, cod, snapper, herring and halibut. Seal meat was prized and the long reefs off both south Cortes and Marina Islands were favourite haulouts for harbour seals. Men used heavy harpoons with detachable points to hunt them from canoes or disguised themselves in sealskin suits to creep up on their prey from shore.

Enough food was gathered and preserved to last through winter. On good years, a surplus was amassed to allow for gift-giving ceremonies to mark births, deaths and marriages, and for trade with other Indigenous groups. The Tla'amin people's trading networks extended more than 500 kilometres (311 miles). Glassy obsidian arrow points found in archaeology digs in this region have been traced to sources as far south as Oregon and as far north as Kingcome Inlet.

Twin was bountiful. The wide tidal flats of Canoe Passage and the islands' rocky ledges were ideal marine habitat. Fast-moving tides oxygenated the waters, enhancing the growth of clams, rockfish, crabs and sea urchins. Migrating salmon passed by, and the deep waters off the south island were a good place to troll for pink salmon. Seals basked on rocky ledges at low tide, and men would have set traps for Twin's many black-tailed deer or worked in pairs to drive them to the shore.

When tree sap flowed in mid-spring, women offered prayers to cedars before pulling strips of bark for use in basketry, clothing and mats. The Tla'amin people had profound respect for nature's bounty, as demonstrated by the word "jej jeh," which translates to both "relatives" and "trees."[15]

"You thank the land the tree sits on," advised Elise Paul of the Tla'amin, "and you offer your thanksgiving in your prayer to the ancestors and to the Creator before you touch that tree, because that tree is a living thing."[16]

In mid-summer, women filled their baskets with bright red huckleberries, which they harvested with combs, later drying the berries in the sun. In

---

15   Sarah Elizabeth Johnson, *A Tla'amin Cultural Landscape: Combining traditional knowledge with archaeological investigation in Grace Harbour, Desolation Sound*, BC.

16   Elsie Paul, as quoted by Lyana Marie Patrick in *Storytelling in the Fourth World: Explorations in Meaning of Place and Tla'amin Resistance to Dispossession* (Victoria: University of Victoria, MA thesis, 1997), p. 48.

CHAPTER TWO

the fall, they cut cattail and tule in marshes like the one at the centre of south Twin, for making household mats and tents.

People living in seasonal camps such as this maintained a careful watch for raiders who captured women and children to trade into slavery. George McGee, a North Coast Salish elder who grew up on Cortes in the 1860s, survived such an attack as a boy by scrambling into the underbrush. The sight of the beheaded corpses of his relatives left McGee with a traumatic memory of how small the men of his family appeared without their heads.

An archaeologist who compiled data about warfare in this region hypothesizes that the Indigenous people had an early warning system, relaying signals from camp to camp, in a sight line from south Cortes, and across Twin to Hernando.[17] Advance warning allowed them to seek refuge. There were two large subterranean houses at Smelt Bay, sunk down to their rafters and camouflaged by a covering of branches and rubble piled on their roofs. On Hernando, three defensive refuges were surrounded by palisades and trenches, where poisoned stakes lay hidden in debris.[18]

But an even more deadly foe arrived on the BC coast in the early 1780s: smallpox. A pandemic swept across North America from colonial forts in Mexico to this part of the coast, even before direct contact with Europeans. It was passed from person to person along Indigenous trade routes. Historical geographers believe its spread stopped in North Coast Salish territory. This pandemic is thought to have killed up to 30 percent of the population.[19]

The first European explorer to reach as far as Tla'amin territory was José Maria Navárez of Spain, aboard the *Santa Saturnina* in 1791. His journals

---

17 William O. Angelbeck, *They Recognize No Superior Chief: Power, Practice, Anarchism and Warfare in the Coast Salish Past.*

18 William O. Angelbeck, *They Recognize No Superior Chief: Power, Practice, Anarchism and Warfare in the Coast Salish Past*, pp. 255–56.

19 Wayne Suttles, editor, *The Handbook of North American Indians* (Washington: Smithsonian Institution, 1990), p. 135, in *Demographic History, 1774–1874*, Robert T. Boyd. In 1792, Europeans saw people in the south Salish Sea area with smallpox scars.

have not survived, but his charts show he reached Texada Island, with a faint outline beyond this sketched in as far as Desolation Sound. The next year, British and Spanish expeditions joined forces to further Navárez's work. Both nations hoped that what's now called the Salish Sea would prove to be the fabled Northwest Passage, a route across North America allowing easier access to trade with Asia.

Their exploration process was laborious. The European ships remained at anchor in protected waters like Spanish Banks, near present-day Vancouver, to await surveyors who charted the region in small, open boats. They'd be gone for up to a week, sleeping and eating on beaches. From Spanish Banks, the surveyors rowed more than 150 kilometres (93 miles) north to Desolation Sound. On return, they recommended the ships make the sound their next base for continued charting.

The four European ships headed north in the rain and wind of a summer squall. "Through this very unpleasant navigation we sailed," wrote Captain George Vancouver of Britain. "About dark we entered [Desolation Sound] and…were driven about as if we were blindfolded in this labyrinth." They dropped anchor off Kinghorn Island, within sight of Twin, buffeted by the wind until past midnight. The next day, the ships sailed several kilometres north to a better anchorage in Teakerne Arm, which became their base for the next two weeks. This protected anchorage is now a popular marine park with a cascading waterfall backed by a lake—but the beauty of the place was lost on Captain Vancouver, who described the whole region as "dreary & gloomy."

On June 27, 1792, Dr. Archibald Menzies of the British expedition joined a small survey crew who mapped what's now Desolation Sound Marine Park. They went ashore near Copplestone Point, where they found a recently abandoned village. "It had been ingeniously engineered as a defensive site," wrote Menzies, "[with] strong scaffolds projecting over the Rock & supporting Houses apparently well [secured]." Menzies and his companions climbed a razorback trail to a drawbridge-like entry point, which allowed them to walk among the house frames of the village—until they found they were covered in fleas. "Myriads of Fleas fixed themselves on our shoes, stockings & clothes in such incredible number that the whole party was obliged to quit the rock in great precipitation," wrote Menzies.

CHAPTER TWO

The British and Spanish captains shared maps, and both gave names to the bays, inlets, and islands they charted, but only a handful of the Spanish place names remain in use. These include Cortes, Marina and Hernando, which were named in honour of Hernán Cortés, the conquistador of Mexico, and his Indigenous slave Marina (or Malinali). Their name for Twin was Ulloa, in honour of Francisco de Ulloa, one of Cortés's commanders, but the name was dropped in the next century.

When the Europeans noticed the tides meet in these waters, they realized they were not in the Northwest Passage. They curtailed their exploration and the British headed north along the east coast of what later came to be called Vancouver Island. In Johnstone Strait, above Quadra Island, Captain Vancouver was surprised to find numerous villages and a much larger Indigenous population compared to what he'd seen to the south. In his published journal, he conjectured the southern waters had been depopulated by a combination of smallpox and warfare.

Captain Vancouver was right on both fronts. By 1792, European traders had been active along Vancouver Island's west coast for several decades. The

In 1792, British explorers marvelled at a recently vacated Indigenous village in Desolation Sound. They toured the site until they found their clothing was covered in fleas, later naming it "Flea Village." NL 0004317 *Ayer Art Digital Collection, Newberry Library*

prized commodity was sea otter pelts, which were exchanged for muskets, nails, beads, blankets and knives. As there were no sea otters along much of Vancouver Island's inner coast, the Kwakwaka'wakw people living just above Salish territory escalated their slave trade, capturing Salish women and children to barter with allies to the north for European goods. This gave the Kwakwaka'wakw people the advantage of earlier access to muskets. They also had a numeric advantage because a smallpox pandemic that swept north in about 1782 killed hundreds of Salish people, but left the Kwakwaka'wakw people unscathed. It appears the spread of the disease was checked by the hazardous waters that form the cultural divide between Kwakwaka'wakw and Salish territories. European trade records of the next few decades document constant attacks by the Kwakwaka'wakw people, who took slaves well into what is now Washington State.

But when smallpox struck once again nearly a century later in 1862, during the colonial era, it hit every part of the BC coast. So many people succumbed that seasonal camps like Twin, and even large winter villages like the one at Smelt Bay, were abandoned. More than 15,000 people are thought to have died in BC in this single outbreak. Gone were leaders and elders, canoe makers, seal hunters, basket makers, singers and memory keepers. The survivors were bereft and demoralized.

Under normal circumstances, death was marked by complex rituals. A deceased person's body was cleansed and dances were performed. Mourners wailed, pulling their hair and beating their breasts. Personal possessions such as cedar bark capes, hats, bone pins and hair combs were burned to send with the dead into the afterlife. Bodies were buried in the clamshell middens of former villages, placed on platforms in trees, or in tombs on small islands, like the one Spanish explorers found in 1792 near the entrance to Desolation Sound.

But the smallpox epidemic of 1862 killed so many people there was no time for ritual. Bodies were simply burnt in heaped pyres on beaches. A shallow mass grave found by settlers at Mansons Landing on Cortes likely relates to smallpox. North Coast Salish elder "Old" George McGee, as he was known to settlers, was one of the few to survive this epidemic. As a boy, he watched helplessly as friends and relatives died on the beach,

CHAPTER TWO

"Old" George McGee of Cortes Island, as this Salish elder was known to settlers, saw relatives die on the beach during the smallpox epidemic of 1862. He also lost family to intertribal warfare during these years, when his people's economy was disrupted by the introduction of European trade. *Museum at Campbell River 19328*

where they'd gone to quell the awful fever of smallpox.[20]

The pandemic had continuing repercussions, leaving survivors with a decreased fertility rate. This perhaps explains why there were no children among the ten adults living in Chief Tom's and Sophie's household in the Twin Islands area at the time of the 1891 census, even though several of the women were of child-bearing age. And smallpox was just one of many diseases this family had faced. Diphtheria, measles, mumps, venereal disease and influenza all had a deadly impact. By 1891, BC's Indigenous population had decreased from the time of first contact with Europeans by more than 80 percent. Settlers predicted that extinction of an entire people—a genocide—would soon be the outcome. Given these circumstances, it's

---

20   Mike Manson's memoirs, BC Archives.

no surprise that places like Twin fell into disuse, leaving it open to be claimed as homestead land by immigrants.

CHAPTER THREE

A Homesteader's Lot

Margaret Nixon embraced the homesteading life of Twin Islands upon moving there in 1912, after she married James Nixon, who was her junior by twenty-five years. *Museum at Campbell River 5444*

By the 1880s, there were a handful of small logging camps and mines on the Discovery Islands, which attracted settlers. Among them was Dan McDonald, or Peg Leg McDonald,[21] as neighbours called him. On July 9, 1889,

---

21   McDonald used many names. According to the 1901 census, he was Donald McDonald. In the 1911 census, his name was spelled Donald Macdonald. His gravestone gives his name as Donald McDonald McArthur.

McDonald registered for a 160-acre[22] (65-hectare) pre-emption on south Twin Island.[23] These land grants were available to British men (and widows) at a dollar an acre, a generous arrangement designed to open agricultural land. Pre-emptors had to live on-site full-time and make "improvements" such as clearing, housing, fencing and ditching. There was no restriction on timing for completion. So long as annual taxes were maintained, the property was effectively theirs. And once the assessed value of improvements had reached a dollar an acre, the settler was eligible for full title.

Land in use by Indigenous people was not open for pre-emption, so presumably there was no longer any sign of active seasonal camps in Canoe Passage. And if any Tla'amin families did happen to stop by after McDonald built his home there, he would have run them off. He'd formed a negative opinion of Indigenous people while living in Wyoming, near the site of General Custer's Last Stand, where the US government lost hundreds of soldiers in its war against Indigenous Americans.[24]

McDonald had immigrated to the US in about 1870 from his home on the remote island of Stornoway, off Scotland's northwest coast.[25] He served on the Liverpool Police Force as a young man, before immigrating first to the US and, a decade later, to Canada.[26] His neighbour on Cortes Island, Rose (Manson) McKay, described him in her memoirs as an irascible but skilled raconteur. As children, she and her siblings could always tell when McDonald was around by the loud tap, tap, tap of his peg leg on wooden floors. He told them he'd lost that leg while buffalo hunting on the Prairies,

---

22 A quarter section, at roughly 160 acres (about 65 hectares), was the upward limit for a pre-emption. Dan McDonald thought he had marked off 160 acres, as he noted on his pre-emption form, but when he had it legally surveyed three decades later, he found it was actually 141 acres (57 hectares).

23 BC Archives GR-2635, Vol. 38, p. 4, shows Dan McDonald registered for Lot 417 on July 9, 1889.

24 Rose (Manson) McKay's memoirs, Museum at Campbell River Archives.

25 Dates for Dan McDonald's birth vary. The 1891 and 1911 censuses give his birth year as 1845, while the 1901 and 1921 censuses give the date as 1851.

26 In the 1901 census, Dan McDonald was said to have immigrated in 1865. The 1901 and 1921 census records, however, say it was 1884.

when his horse stepped into a gopher hole and fell on him. He was 145 kilometres (90 miles) away from the nearest doctor, and by the time he reached help, the doctor concluded that amputation was the only option. Later, McDonald would grow angry every time he told this story, convinced the doctor could have saved his leg.

McDonald sometimes worked on Cortes Island's road-building crew. When he did, he camped on John and Margaret Manson's farm, which was on a high bluff overlooking Twin. "It was exciting to see his campfire in the evening," wrote Rose (Manson) McKay. She and her siblings scampered across the field to enjoy a slice of McDonald's bannock, made in a large frying pan, and to hear stories of his adventures as a Liverpool policeman and a cowboy on the American plains.

It was likely the loss of his leg that brought Dan McDonald to the BC coast to raise sheep, because he could no longer ride a horse. In doing so, he was returning to the work of his youth. McDonald was about forty years old and still in his prime when he cleared land for a pasture and an orchard on sloping land above Canoe Passage. He built a one-room cabin above the beach, but instead of placing the logs horizontally as others did, he stood his up vertically, perhaps to make it easier for a one-legged man to maneuver. The resulting house was a low rectangle with a couple of narrow windows tucked under the eaves, reminiscent in shape and size to the crofter's huts of his youth. McDonald added a bumped-up second storey at one end, presumably for a loft bedroom, and spruced up the interior with wallpaper, its delicate floral pattern following the contour of the logs.

McDonald augmented sheep farming with seasonal roadwork on Cortes. He let his flock roam Twin freely until the driest part of summer, when he loaded them into his rowboat to relocate to a meadow on Cortes, one boatload at a time.[27] Later yet he hefted them back onboard to sell "on the hoof" to the region's logging and mining camps, sometimes travelling as far as 50 kilometres (31 miles).[28]

---

27   Charlie Allen's diaries, Cortes Museum.
28   In the 1890s, a short-lived gold rush town called Shoal Bay (north of Bute Inlet) provided a market for produce grown by Discovery Islanders.

A HOMESTEADER'S LOT

By the early 1890s, there were small post offices and stores at government docks on Cortes, across the channel at Lund and on Hernando. There were about ten immigrant families living on Hernando, which was an anomaly at a time when the settler population was otherwise dominated by single men. But when the Union Steamship Company of Vancouver started delivering mail and freight along the inner coast in 1892, it brought an influx of newcomers, including a few women and children. The start of scheduled freight and passenger service provided weekly deliveries, and settlers like McDonald could now order tea, coffee, sugar, flour, dried fruit, lamp oil, fabric and boots from stores in Vancouver.

Among the new arrivals was William Jones, who bought all 94 hectares (232 acres) of north Twin from the government. Purchasing this land bypassed pre-emption requirements for full-time residency, a move usually employed by those intending to log rather than homestead. But in this case, there's no on-site evidence of any sort of development.[29] He had a plan, however, for this and several other nearby properties, which he bought on the cusp of a deep recession that struck in 1893. And he hung onto north Twin for more than a decade.[30]

With only the absent William Jones as a neighbour, Dan McDonald was often lonely, as he told a friend on Cortes.[31] In the summer of 1912, after twenty-three years on Twin, McDonald moved to Cortes, where he became the foreman of a road building crew. He was in his mid-sixties and ready for change.[32]

---

29 BC Lands Branch, Victoria, BC. Jones also bought several other properties on the Sunshine Coast at this same time, likely intending to log.

30 William Jones was living in southeastern BC when he lost title to north Twin in 1906 for defaulting on tax payment, according to BC Lands Branch records. There's no further information about this man, though there was a widower listed as W.H. Jones in the Nelson directory from 1901 to 1910. This man worked as a hotel clerk and later as a job printer.

31 Charlie Allen's diary, Cortes Museum. In October 1905, McDonald told Allen he wanted to give up raising sheep.

32 In Charlie Allen's diary, he noted on February 26, 1913, that McDonald was now the

CHAPTER THREE

That same summer, on August 7, 1912, Reverend Harpur Colville Nixon registered for a pre-emption in south Twin's Echo Bay (then called Garden Bay). He had little in common with Twin's first settler. While McDonald was a stocky, sociable man with rough edges and opinions, Reverend Nixon was a tall, lanky fellow with a prodigious beard and a "mingling taste for scholarship and a life in the wilds," as he was described in a local newspaper. He was an ordained minister in name only, having taken holy orders only to fulfill inheritance requirements for his father's large estate in Northern Ireland.[33]

Reverend Nixon's pre-emption was the largest on south Twin. It was an ideal base from which to pursue his passion for hunting and fishing trips aboard his small yacht, *Salal*. He'd recently separated from his wife and had signed over title to their farm on Denman Island, about 90 kilometres (56 miles) to the south. All but the youngest of his six sons were adults by this time, and his second son, James, had recently married.

James and his bride, Margaret, soon joined Reverend Nixon on Twin, taking over Dan McDonald's old cabin in Canoe Passage. And before the year was out, Reverend Nixon arranged to purchase this property.[34]

His next move was to build a large house for himself in Echo Bay, where he cleared about 3.5 hectares (9 acres) for livestock and a garden. The south-facing slope overlooked Baker Passage and the beaches and bluffs of Hernando, which had largely been abandoned by the settlers of several decades before. Just a few Tla'amin families still came there to fish in summer.

The isolation of their new home suited James and Margaret Nixon. In 1913, James pre-empted a lot on the west flank of McDonald's former

---

foreman of their road crew. The exact date McDonald relocated to Cortes is not known. He did not process the paperwork required to get full title to his Twin Islands homestead until December 30, 1912 (BC Archives, GR 2635) and it was yet another year before the property deed was transferred to Reverend Nixon's name.

33   *Victoria Daily Times*, August 9, 1915, p. 13.

34   Dan McDonald didn't secure full title to his pre-emption until December 3, 1912, after which Reverend Nixon could officially purchase the property. Their friend Rose (Manson) McKay understood Nixon purchased this homestead as a wedding gift for his son James, but BC Lands Branch records show that Reverend Nixon retained title to this property.

The eccentric Reverend Nixon (left, with Nicol Manson) became an ordained minister to fulfill inheritance requirements for his father's large estate in Northern Ireland. With him here are his son James and daughter-in-law Margaret, along with Anna and Jack Manson of Cortes Island. *Museum at Campbell River 19,267*

homestead in Canoe Passage. He built a small shack there, as survey records show, and cleared enough land to fulfill pre-emption requirements—though he and Margaret continued to live on McDonald's former homestead.

McDonald's rudimentary cabin, with its stained and peeling wallpaper, was a less-than-idyllic honeymoon retreat, but James's photographs capture the couple's delight in each other and in their new home. His pictures also form a visual record of their many activities. Each photograph was carefully staged. In some, Margaret and James sit indoors, reading or drinking tea. In one, Margaret wears a crisp white dress with a bow tie at the neck, gesticulating toward four pig carcasses hanging to cure. Later, she poses outside McDonald's cabin, holding strings of plump sausages and a plate of pork pie. They were living almost exclusively from the bounty of the land and sea, preserving fruit, raising poultry, hunting deer and geese, and fishing from a kayak-shaped boat called *Twin*.

When Margaret and James appear together in these photographs, they gaze fondly into each other's eyes. They were clearly in love, though they were an unconventional couple by the standards of any day. James was 23

CHAPTER THREE

James Nixon's photographs lovingly document the life he and his wife Margaret led together on Twin Islands. *Cortes Museum and Archives 2004.002.054001*

and Margaret was a 48-year-old widow[35] when they were married on June 6, 1912. It's likely they met through friends or at church in Vancouver, which was then James's port of call as a steamship engineer.

Margaret had been convalescing from surgery when they were married—so she told Rose (Manson) McKay of Cortes Island. She said she'd "inhaled" a parasite while living in India, where she and her first husband had been medical missionaries.[36] Doctors had tried unsuccessfully to remove the parasite, leaving her with a heavily scarred left cheek. After her

---

35   Margaret Jane Street grew up in a large family in Wednesbury, Staffordshire, England, where her father was a colliery engineer. She and a sister went to India as medical missionaries. After her first husband died, Margaret returned to England, then immigrated to Canada, where a sister lived. On her marriage certificate, she said Toronto was her home, but she'd been living in Vancouver for several years. Margaret's name could not, however, be found in the 1911 Canadian census. Nor does her name appear in the Vancouver directory.

36   Margaret Street married John Butler in Bombay in 1896, according to online records for India. The Mansons of Cortes understood she had two children by that first marriage, and that they had died, but no record of them is available.

A HOMESTEADER'S LOT

Reverend Nixon's new bungalow in Canoe Passage was considered excessive by local standards of the time. It had five rooms and cost $4,000 to build. *Marian (Andrews) Harrison collection, courtesy John Harrison*

first husband died of a fever in 1901, Margaret returned home to England, where she worked as a cook for a cotton manufacturer for a time.[37] In about 1910, she followed a sister to Ontario; and later, on a visit to Vancouver, she met and married James Nixon.

In 1914, Reverend Nixon replaced McDonald's cabin with a five-room bungalow described by a local newspaper as a "very pretentious summer home." It cost $4,000,[38] the equivalent of about four years' wages for the average working family. The property and the new house remained in his name, suggesting he built it to induce his son and daughter-in-law to stay, but considered it a personal investment.

In October 1914, the Nixons learned a man named John Maclellan Mackinnon had bought north Twin for the price of unpaid back taxes, at $766.[39] Mackinnon was a self-made man. He'd started out as a homesteader

---

37 Information courtesy of Margaret Thomson, a descendant of Margaret Nixon's birth family.

38 *Vancouver Daily World*, January 6, 1921, p. 6.

39 While the record of this purchase is on file at the BC Lands Branch, Mackinnon's name was not fully processed as the owner, perhaps because his ownership was so short.

but had struck it rich with a gold mine north of Vancouver in the 1890s. Reverend Nixon was clearly annoyed that someone had scooped up this property because just eight days later, he swung a deal to buy north Twin from Mackinnon.[40]

With this purchase, Reverend Nixon now owned three of Twin's five lots, and James held a fourth as a pre-emption. They must have had plans to buy Twin's fifth and final lot on the southeast corner of Canoe Passage as well, but fate intervened.

Their troubles started with a decline in Margaret Nixon's health in 1915, forcing her and James to move in with his mother on Denman Island. Reverend Nixon's middle son, Louis, moved to Twin for a time, but soon left to work in Lund.

The night he left, on July 6, 1915, Reverend Nixon followed his usual evening ritual, lounging on his bunk aboard the *Salal* to read by the light of a battery-operated lamp and enjoy a final pipe. He was on his own on the islands now. He must have kept one ear cocked for the sound of the wind dragging against the anchor chain, because there was a southeast storm blowing that night. He reached into a pouch he kept in his shirt pocket for a pinch of tobacco to fill his pipe, and then he lit it. As he did so, a "violent explosion" struck him in the face. The blast tore away part of his jaw and knocked Reverend Nixon unconscious, said a newspaper report.

When he came to, he was in pain and shock, but still able to seek help. "Realizing that I would not have strength to do much if I did not hurry, I rowed to the launch and started the boat for Manson's," Reverend Nixon later wrote. The launch had a motor, so he reached Margaret and John Manson's farm within minutes, pushed by the storm through a lumpy sea. The injured man climbed the Mansons' steep bluff, with a towel pressed against his bleeding jaw. Margaret Manson was the first to awake at his approach, his muffled calls for help sounding to her like a drunken reveller. She waited behind their closed front door and dashed it open just as Reverend Nixon approached, flashing a torchlight into his face. "The sight was so horrible," an investigating constable later wrote, "she ran shrieking to her nearest

---

40   This man, or another with a similar name, age, and country of origin, lived near Dan McDonald at the time of the 1891 census.

neighbour." Meanwhile, her husband, John, arose and came to Nixon's aid—bandaging him as best he could. Nixon hastily wrote a simple will and a short account of what had happened on scraps of paper, saying he thought a .22 cartridge had somehow got into the bowl of his pipe. It—or perhaps his lighter—had exploded.

John Manson took Reverend Nixon to Lund, mindful of his instructions to spare his new engine by running it at half throttle. They arrived in Lund at about midnight, and Manson turned Reverend Nixon over to his son Louis's care. Louis took his father to a doctor in nearby Powell River, but the case was so severe the doctor referred them on to Vancouver, where they arrived at 3 a.m.[41]

Reverend Nixon had been so sure his injury was due to his own error, his neighbours didn't report the accident to police for several days. But when they checked the yacht, they found the bowl of his pipe lying intact on the floor. Reverend Nixon had not been injured by a blast from his pipe. An investigating officer later deduced he was shot by a high-calibre rifle. Evidence showed a bullet had entered through a porthole, striking Reverend Nixon in the jaw, then slicing across his pillow and pinning a circular tuft of feathers into the opposite wall. The direction of blood splatters on this wall and on the floor suggested the shooter had been either on a boat of about the same height as the *Salal*, or on the adjacent bluff.

The constable interviewed neighbours, including a Tla'amin family camped on Hernando. The details he gathered assured him that while Reverend Nixon was an eccentric man who was estranged from his wife, he had no known enemies. The constable's theory was that Reverend Nixon was shot in error by a "pit-lamper," someone using a bright light to catch the reflective shine of an animal's eyes, transfixing it for just long enough to get a shot. Most area residents relied on wild game for food, so laws against this practice were loosely enforced. "This may sound far-fetched," wrote the constable, "but it is well-known that the average pit-lamper will fire at any light he happens to come near."

Reverend Nixon agreed with this theory. "A considerable number of pit-lampers come hanging around and have already given trouble stealing

---

41   Inquest into Reverend Nixon's death, BC Archives, 241/1915.

sheep and killing them, and [I] have had to see the police before," he wrote from his hospital bed. "You ask Mr. Manson how they have killed his sheep. And if I get well, I shall not take any action," he added, "to bring any man to justice."

Nixon remained in hospital nearly a month, living on a liquid diet. In August, he decided to undergo reconstructive surgery. His doctor warned him he may not survive in his weakened condition, but he preferred that risk to a life as "a pup-fed" invalid. The day before his surgery, Reverend Nixon signed off on a detailed will, leaving his investments and a 3,700-hectare (9,350-acre) estate in Ireland to his eldest son. He left his three lots on Twin to his youngest child, ten-year-old John, as an investment to help pay for the boy's education.

Reverend Nixon did not survive surgery. When his death was announced in the media, an old friend from Ireland told a Vancouver newspaper about a "singular coincidence." Nixon's father had survived a similar injury, having been shot in the jaw by Irish rebels in 1858. Several men dressed as women had seized the reins of the family's carriage horses, while another stuck a pistol through the window and fired point-blank at Reverend Nixon's father. His mother shoved the muzzle of the pistol aside just in time to deflect what would have otherwise been a fatal shot. He was left with nothing more serious than the loss of some teeth.

To this day, Reverend Harpur Nixon's oddly similar injury, and subsequent death, remains a mystery. About a decade after his death, a rifle with a burnt stock and a rusty barrel was found on a bluff opposite where the *Salal* had been moored the night he was shot. An owner could not be traced because the serial numbers were no longer legible.

With several homesteads, two substantial houses, barns and livestock, Twin Islands attracted pillagers. An area resident was caught stealing doors, windows and "other parts" from the bungalow in Canoe Passage, which was out-of-view of caretaker Thomas Sutton, who had moved into Reverend Nixon's house in Echo Bay.[42]

---

42 *Vancouver Daily World*, January 14, 1921, reported the theft of property on Twin by Chris Hagan. Little is known of the elderly bachelor Thomas Sutton, who lived in Reverend Nixon's former home in Echo Bay. He remained on the island for 17 years, until the time of his death in 1932.

A HOMESTEADER'S LOT

More trouble lay ahead for the Nixon family during these years. Hundreds of Canada's young men were dying in the trenches and mud of France during World War I, but James Nixon was not conscripted, likely because he was working on his mother's farm on Denman Island, which was considered an essential service. This was a blessing for his wife, Margaret, whose illness grew increasingly worse. In March 1917, she was hospitalized in Vancouver. Friends on Cortes heard that Margaret died on the operating table as doctors made a final attempt to remove the parasite she'd acquired in India.

But Margaret's death certificate tells a different story.[43] The malady that killed her was syphilis. Her symptoms, including the damage to her nasal passages and cheek, which she'd claimed were the result of a previous surgery, are typical of the degradation of syphilis. Her death must have been a disfiguring and painful descent into madness. We'll never know how she contracted this disease, but it's likely to have been through her first husband, who she always claimed had "died of a fever." (It also appears that she and James took precautions to ensure he did not contract the disease, because he went on to live into old age.)

Just months after Margaret's death, James Nixon enlisted in the Canadian Navy. While stationed in Bermuda,[44] he met his second wife, Grace Holman, and they were married following the war, on January 27, 1919. They made Vancouver their home, and James worked as a mechanic.[45] About a year later, he completed the paperwork to get full title to his pre-emption on south Twin,[46] in readiness to sell. His eldest brother, as executor, likewise

---

43   For reasons unknown, James registered his wife's name as "Marjorie" Nixon, rather than Margaret, in both her death certificate and in a newspaper obituary.

44   Rose (Manson) McKay understood James's second wife to have been from the Bahamas, but her death certificate shows she was born in Bermuda to English and Anglo-Indian parents. See also 1921 census.

45   James Nixon died in 1977 in Sardis, BC. The couple did not have children. Neither suffered from syphilis, the painful and disfiguring disease that killed Margaret Nixon.

46   James Nixon had not fulfilled pre-emption requirements for full-time residency, but he applied for clemency in light of his war service, which was accepted. See BC Lands Branch records.

CHAPTER THREE

Margaret Nixon often posed for her husband's photographs with her damaged cheek facing away from the camera. She said the scar was caused by surgery, in a failed attempt to remove a parasite she'd inhaled in India, but her death certificate tells another story—Margaret died of syphilis. *Cortes Museum 2004.002.037001*

arranged to sell their father's lots on Twin, on behalf of their youngest brother, John. It was a slow process. "Negotiations were concluded in chancery court today for the sale of Twin Islands," announced the *Vancouver Daily World* on January 6, 1921. "Twin Islands [is] one of the prettiest properties on the coast."

The new owners, Joseph and Clara McCauley, bought all four lots from the Nixons. They broke with tradition in this purchase by registering the deed in both their names, at a time when property ownership was still considered to be an exclusively male privilege. But, as the couple had no children, they had both saved earnings from work in logging camps on the Sunshine Coast.

Joseph McCauley's 13-year-old niece, Dorothy, had recently become their ward and she joined them on Twin. She was still in school, according to the 1921 census,[47] so she either continued her studies by correspondence

---

47 Dorothy Lorraine Poquette was a niece to Joseph McCauley. Her father (a Seattle barber) was still alive, but the McCauleys raised her from the age of ten and she took their surname.

Dorothy (McCauley) Nash (right) was raised on Twin Islands and likely boated across to Cortes to attend school with her friend Rose (Manson) McKay. They're seen here on a visit to Vancouver. *Cortes Museum and Archives 2007.001.539*

CHAPTER THREE

or rowed across to Cortes and hiked the trail from the Mansons' farm to attend that community's one-room school.

Homesteading was nothing new for the McCauleys, who had previously farmed in the Powell River area and, before that, in Washington State. Like other Twin Islanders before them, sheep farming became their mainstay. To improve upon Twin's flock of feral sheep, the McCauleys got a government grant to buy sixty purebred ewes and a ram from Alberta.[48]

Purchasing Twin at this time was impressive, given a deep recession that caused many bankruptcies throughout the region. The Hard Times, as this period was called, was the result of the high cost of World War 1—and there were more bankruptcies on this part of the coast at this time than during the Great Depression that followed. Some families had to send their children to orphanages in Vancouver because they couldn't afford to clothe and feed them. Even the cost of a simple pair of canvas shoes was out of reach for many until the economy began to lift in about 1924. It was at this point that the McCauleys bought the fifth lot—making them the first to own Twin Islands in its entirety.[49]

Clara McCauley and her niece, Dorothy, were especially fond of Twin. "A couple of years after we'd purchased the Twins, we had a very attractive offer to sell," Dorothy later wrote. "By [then] my aunt and I had become very attached to the lonely, enchanted isles, and I, a pre-teen youngster, was so upset at the thought of parting, that the offer was turned down."[50]

The McCauleys augmented their farm income with selective logging on the islands through the 1920s.[51] Their crew included a young man named Dick Nash, who had a homestead in Theodosia Arm, near Lund. He courted Dorothy, boating across the channel several times a week to visit after he'd finished logging on Twin. They were married in Powell River in 1932.

With Dorothy gone, life became difficult for Clara McCauley, who suffered from a chronic respiratory illness. She died on October 24, 1936, just

---

48 *Vancouver Sun,* July 29, 1922.
49 The McAuleys purchased Lot 1046 on April 25, 1924, according to BC Lands Branch records.
50 Dorothy (McCauley) Nash, *History of Twin Islands,* courtesy Julie Neal.
51 Dorothy (McCauley) Nash, *History of Twin Islands.*

days after she and her husband sold Twin. Losing the islands was devastating for Clara. "If it were scientifically possible that one could die of a broken heart," said the attending physician, "this would be such an instance."

Joseph McCauley remained on the BC coast after his wife's death and kept abreast of changes on Twin. When he died several decades later, his obituary said one of his proudest achievements was being the first to own all of Twin Islands.

Dorothy (McCauley) Nash[52] made friends with at least one of Twin's caretakers over the following years, which allowed her to revisit its forested trails, cliffs and coves—the secret places of her childhood—and to watch as Twin was transformed from a subsistence homestead into a resort for the wealthy.

---

52 Dorothy (McCauley) Nash's descendants could not be traced. Her only child, a card shark who made his living identifying cheaters in casinos, died prematurely and was estranged from his family.

CHAPTER FOUR

Asian Roots

In 1936, Dick and Ethel Andrews, American expats living in Japan, hired an agent to find them a remote island on the BC coast. They wanted a place with great fishing, moorage, a reliable water source and arable land—a haven from a second global war, which Dick Andrews predicted was on the horizon. They were still in Japan when their agent bought Twin Islands on October 24, 1936. He'd chosen well, as they found on their first visit about six weeks later. Their arrival was a major turning point for Twin, which was to become a focal investment for wealth the Andrews family had amassed as industrial machinery merchants over the past three decades.

Richard Magill (Dick) Andrews was born in Cincinnati, Ohio, on August 6, 1885. When he was five, his father became the United States' senior vice consul in China. When he was ten, the family moved to Japan, where his father and a friend[53] started an import business—Andrews & George—barging in loads of American steel and machine-made goods such as motor parts, mining and milling machinery, safes, typewriters, motorcycles, cars, motorboats and tractors. Andrews & George also later manufactured hard-to-find components like airplane spark plugs and magnetos.[54] "The Japanese

---

53 According to descendant John Harrison, Henry Andrews established Andrews & George with Edward W. George in 1894.

54 See *Los Angeles Times*, October 7, 1922; John Harrison interview, October 21, 2017; and *Japan Times*, October 18, 1921. Andrews & George is thought to have imported the first motorcar to Japan in about 1902.

US citizen, Richard Magill (Dick) Andrews, became a multimillionaire, based upon the success of his import business in Japan, but he lost much of his fortune when he and his family had to flee to Canada on the cusp of WWII. *R.M. Andrews III collection, courtesy Wendy Andrews*

CHAPTER FOUR

put much of the machinery and tools to use in their munitions factories," says a family history,[55] since Japan was at war with China through much of the early twentieth century.

Though he had lived in the far east for most of his childhood, Dick Andrews was still very much an American. After finishing school in Japan, he attended college in Michigan, where he got an engineering degree. While there, he met Ethel Hosking, the daughter of an English immigrant who owned a successful dry-goods and hardware store.[56] On returning to Asia for a job with an American gold-mining company in Korea, Dick proposed to Ethel by post.[57]

Ethel Hosking had wanted to become a doctor, but women of her generation were discouraged from entering this—or any—profession. Instead, she had travelled alone to France as a young woman and stayed there with a family for a year.[58] Now, at the age of 24, Ethel prepared for her marriage to Dick Andrews. She assembled "one of the most gorgeous trousseaus to ever leave Los Angeles," said a newspaper in 1909. Ethel's father escorted her by ship from Los Angeles to San Francisco, where she was to board an ocean liner for Japan. She brought a trunk and several leather boxes filled with a "shimmering, satiny bridal gown, with a dainty veil and yards of priceless

---

55   *The Harrisons, 1890–1990*, p. 5, a self-published family history based upon interviews with Marian (Andrews) Harrison and her husband, Slim Harrison, courtesy John Harrison. Much of their imports wound up in munitions, says this source. As Japan's demands for weapons increased, so did their need for machinery and tools to make them. Consequently, Andrews & George prospered. However, as advertisements in the *Japan Times* show, they also stocked general merchandise.

56   US 1900 census; and R.M. (Bill) Andrews's personal papers dated April 19, 1993, courtesy Wendy Andrews.

57   *Los Angeles Times*, November 21, 1909, announced Dick Andrews's and Ethel Hosking's forthcoming wedding. Dick Andrews was associated with the Oriental Gold Mining Company of Korea, said this source. According to *The Harrisons, 1890–1990*, Dick's father hoped he would become the manager of this mine.

58   Email communication from Dick and Ethel Andrews's granddaughter Jenny (Harrison) Young, July 8, 2018.

HER ROMANCE COMPLICATED.

Loses Trousseau and Gifts in Steamer Fire.

Los Angeles Girl on Way to Her Wedding Halted.

Cablegram to Japan Delays the Ceremony.

The fire that totally destroyed the steamship St. Croix Saturday afternoon and endangered the lives of the 178 men and women on board, spoiled for a time the pretty romance of Miss Ethel D. Hosking, of No. 664 Benton boulevard.

Miss Hosking was on board the steamer, accompanied by her father. She was en route to San Francisco, there to sail on the Manchuria to Yokohama, Japan, where she was to be married to Richard McGill Andrews, son of former United States Minister to Japan, on December 14.

Instead of happy anticipations of the wedding and the honeymoon, Miss Hosking spent the greater part of the cold night on the desolate shores of the upper Malibu, while the waves and the night wind sobbed a requiem over the blackened hulk of the St. Croix, and the passengers huddled about the fire, staring fearfully into the night and thinking of what might have happened.

On board the steamer Miss Hosking had an elaborate trousseau and in her trunk were presents valued at more than $1500. Cut glass, silver and gold ornaments and a host of other pretty trinkets, tributes of the love and well wishes of the young woman's scores of friends in Los Angeles, had been carefully packed in the bottom of one of the big trunks. The other leather boxes were crammed with one of the most gorgeous trousseaus that ever went out of Los Angeles. Everything that a young girl desires in the way of pretty clothes was there, and most beautiful of al, the shimmering, satiny bridal gown with its dainty veil and its yards of priceless lace.

So that it was no wonder that the young bride-to-be sat disconsolately upon the rocky shore, while the night winds caught and whipped about the stray tendrils of hair that slipped loose from beneath her net.

Instead of a comfortable, happy trip to San Francisco, the first step of that long voyage that was to carry her to her life's happiness, she had faced death by fire and drowning, she had been thoroughly soaked in the fog and surf, her clothes had been ruined,

Miss Ethel Haskins,

who lost her trousseau and $1500 worth of wedding presents on the ill-fated St. Croix. She was on her way to Japan to be married.

Ethel Hosking was interviewed by the Los Angeles Times in 1909, after she was shipwrecked off the California coast at the outset of her journey to Japan to be married to Dick Andrews. Her lavish trousseau, wedding dress and gifts sank with the ship. Los Angeles Times, November 22, 1909

CHAPTER FOUR

lace," and $1,500 worth of cut glass, silver and gold wedding gifts.[59] Within an hour of departure, the *St. Croix* caught fire and the blaze shot up through the centreboard and into the masts. The captain ordered evacuation, starting with women and children, and steered toward shore in a thick winter fog—but Ethel chose to remain with her father. They were among the last to be ferried ashore through breakers to a rocky beach.

Several crew members set off in search of help, leaving Ethel, her father and the other passengers huddled around bonfires in their wet clothing, watching as the *St. Croix* burned to the waterline and sank. In the morning, ranchers and townsfolk from Santa Monica, about 29 kilometres (18 miles) distant, escorted them along the beach in tippy mule carts. Though they were exhausted, wet and hungry, most preferred to walk.

According to the *Los Angeles Times*, Ethel Hosking lost everything, but within days she again set off for Japan. In her letters home, Ethel said little about the wreck of the *St. Croix*, focusing instead on the details of her wedding, which took place in Yokohama, Tokyo's port city. She and Dick exchanged vows beneath a giant paper bell in a private residence decorated in white and green on December 14, 1909. Her replacement gown had a deeply pointed princess-line bodice and lace train, and Dick looked "swell" in a double-breasted frock coat that hung below the knee.

"Well, here we are, a 48-hours-old married couple," wrote Ethel from their honeymoon suite. "It is absolutely no use trying to tell you how happy I am, dears, for that would be impossible." In contrast to Ethel's loose scrawl, Dick added a note in an old-fashioned copperplate script. "I thought I should like to write a few lines to tell you how happy I am with Ethel beside me at last," he wrote.

These letters are some of the few personal records that have survived, leaving us to guess at the Andrews family's views and values. Their story, related here, has been pieced together from family anecdotes and public records. Travel documents show that Ethel was a petite 157 centimetres (5 feet 2 inches) tall, and a head shorter than Dick, at 178 centimetres (5 feet 10 inches). They both had blue eyes and sandy hair, and they both

---

59   *Los Angeles Times*, November 22, 1909, p. 5. This would have been the equivalent of a generous annual income.

loved animals. Dick was especially fond of dogs and birds. When I visited their grandson John Harrison at his Andrews & George office in Vancouver in the summer of 2018, a waggling dog followed at our heels as he showed me his many Japanese heirlooms, including Dick Andrews's former desk.[60] When asked about the images of birds that grace his walls, Harrison flashed a broad smile. "I'm sure I have every book ever published about North American birds," he said. It was a passion that had earned him the teasing moniker of "The Bird Man."

I saw Harrison's older cousin, Dick Andrews Junior, later that same day, a visit that took on poignancy because he died unexpectedly just a few months later. This Dick Andrews was the third in line to bear the name Richard Magill Andrews. For the sake of clarity, the family patriarch is referred to here as Dick Andrews, his son as Bill,[61] and his grandson as Dick Junior.

Dick Junior, his wife, Joan, and their daughter, Wendy (the family historian), greeted me at the door of their home, across Burrard Inlet from the Andrews & George office. Boxes were stacked in the far corners in readiness for a move to a condominium, but their many Japanese treasures still graced the walls. Among them were images of birds. Dick Junior's father had gained notoriety in Japan for his love of birds—and because he introduced Canada geese into Asia.

Wendy took charge of an energetic young dog that wedged itself between our knees and the coffee table, and her father slid into his deep recliner with a gracious smile. Dick Junior bore a striking resemblance to his grandfather. He also shared his grandfather's enthusiasm for nature and fishing. Both Dick Junior and his cousin John Harrison had similar recollections of their grandparents. Ethel's meals were memorable, and she liked to make things with her hands. She tied fishing flies and knit and

---

60   John's father, Slim Harrison, revived the Vancouver-based Andrews & George business after a brief hiatus, specializing in Japanese tea imports.

61   Dick Andrews's mother intercepted registration papers for the birth of his first two children and changed their names. So, while Dick and Ethel chose the name William (Bill) for their son, he was officially registered under the name Richard, hence his confusing array of names.

CHAPTER FOUR

The Andrews family lived in Korea for the first decade of their married life, while Dick worked as an engineer in a mine. Ethel Andrews sits in the back seat (left) with, perhaps, a nanny. Dick Andrews sits on the front (right) with their son Bill on his knee. *R.M. Andrews III collection, courtesy Wendy Andrews*

embroidered bed coverings, many of which remained in use for more than six decades in the lodge she and her husband built on Twin. Their grandfather also had a creative side, which showed up in his designs for jewellery, rugs, light fixtures and furniture. Ethel was kindly, though reserved, but their grandfather had a ready smile, which one newspaper reporter described as a puckish grin. That grin hinted at an impetuous streak that caught people off guard, like the time a visiting American official made offensive comments at the dinner table. The content of his remarks is lost, but Dick Andrews rose from the table and returned astride his horse, which he rode down the hallway of their summer home, through the kitchen and around the dining room table, causing their unwelcome guest to leave.[62]

Ethel Andrews liked to tell her grandchildren stories from her first decade of married life, when she and Dick lived in Korea. Dick had travelled ahead to prepare their four-room cottage in an American compound,

---

62   *The Harrisons, 1890–1990.*

leaving Ethel to follow. She was pushed through the mountains in a wheelbarrow that tipped several times, spilling Ethel and her bags into the surrounding rice paddies. The mine site itself, as contemporary pictures show, was a steeply terraced hillside of rubble, with miners' cottages, slag heaps and the smoking plume of an industrial building in the valley below. Dick and his four dogs greeted Ethel on arrival. He'd prepared a bathtub for her, welding metal oil drums together. Unfortunately, the white paint was still fresh, so when Ethel slipped into her luxurious bath her bottom stuck to the tub.

Ethel had experienced cold winters in Michigan, so she was prepared for Korea's heavy snow and sub-zero temperatures. Weeks of freezing weather allowed miners to hang venison carcasses from their eaves and cut slabs of meat as needed. It was into this wasteland of slag heaps and snow that their son, Richard Magill Andrews Junior (known as Bill), was born on December 14, 1910. There was no doctor available, so Dick and a servant were Ethel's only attendants. Their second child, Elizabeth Ann, followed in 1913. Shortly thereafter, the Andrews family moved to Japan,[63] where Dick joined his father's import firm. And six years later, when his father died in 1919, Dick became the sole owner-operator of Andrews & George.

It was a turbulent time—politically, professionally, and personally—to take over the family business. Though the country had adopted democratic rule when Andrews & George was first established in the 1890s, the Japanese military had gradually regained power. Foreigners like the Andrews were not readily accepted, but the military had become increasingly reliant on Andrews & George for steel imports, so they were tolerated—but not trusted. "I am afraid that all American firms are going to have hard sledding for a few months at least, [because] feeling is extremely bitter," wrote one of Andrews & George's American secretaries in a letter home in the 1920s. "The newspapers print all kinds of inflammatory articles and there

---

63 Descendant Jenny (Harrison) Young, email communication, said the Andrews family moved to Japan in 1913; a date also noted in a letter Bill Andrews wrote on November 16, 1964, courtesy Wendy Andrews. However, in another document, Bill Andrews said his family moved to Japan in 1915. In *The Harrisons, 1890–1990*, the date given for this move was 1914.

are innumerable mass meetings and especially gatherings of students, who seem to be always looking for something to make a demonstration about."[64] She said a boycott of American goods was being considered, rocks were hurled at Americans in their cars, expats were refused service in some of Tokyo's shops, and the hotels they frequented stopped holding dances.

Dick and Ethel's third and last child, Marian, was born at the start of the decade. Just months later, in November 1920,[65] their middle child, Elizabeth Ann, died at the age of seven,[66] causing Ethel's hair to turn prematurely gray. The next year, when the family's Chinese nursemaid lay dying, Ethel agreed to take care of the woman's teenage daughter.[67] Dick and Ethel legally adopted Tonie Wong—a bright young woman who they sent to business college in the US. Doing so caused a stir in the US media, where Dick and Ethel were otherwise largely unknown. "Miss Tonie Wong, a Chinese orphan, is to become Americanized, as the ward of W.H. Hosking [Ethel's father], a New York businessman," announced newspapers across the country. And later still, when Wong became Dick Andrews's personal secretary, there were rumours he was her biological father. (His son, Bill, countered this rumour in a memoir, pointing out his father had been in college in the US when Tonie Wong was born in Japan.)[68]

Tonie faced racism on two fronts when she returned to Japan. US expats viewed themselves as a cut above Asians, and her English-and-Chinese origins were disdained by Japanese people. But Tonie's charm and confidence overcame such prejudices. She became a sought-after member of Japan's

---

64 It's not clear when Edward George, a business partner of the Andrews, died. One source says 1913. Family historian Wendy Andrews believes he died in 1916; but in *The Harrisons, 1890–1990*, p. 57, he was said to have died in 1919.

65 Wendy Andrews's family tree.

66 Several records, including *The Harrisons, 1890–1990*, say the child died from meningitis, but family historian Wendy Andrews believes it was mastoiditis, a bacterial infection in the bone behind the ears.

67 According to Jenny (Harrison) Young, in an email dated July 17, 2018, Tonie Wong's biological father died prematurely, so she took the surname of her Chinese stepfather, who also died prematurely.

68 Bill Andrews's personal papers, courtesy Wendy Andrews.

CHINESE BARBERS BUSY BOBBING HAIR OF FLAPPERS, declares Miss Tonie Wong, Chinese orphan ward of W. M. Hoskins, New York business man, who has reached San Francisco on her way to metropolis to continue her education. (Int'l Newsreel)

The Andrews family adopted Tonie Wong after the death of her mother, who was one of their servants. They sent the bright young woman to a business college in the US, which caused a flurry of reportage in newspapers across the country. *Evening Report, Lebanon, Pennsylvania, March 18, 1924*

business and social elite, joining the afternoon bridge parties that were de rigueur among expats. Her broad network of friends would later prove valuable when the Andrews family was forced to leave Japan.

Andrews & George continued to grow through the 1920s, despite the many personal and professional difficulties the family faced early in this decade. They converted a former temple into a fine new home in Tokyo and, in 1922,[69] they built a summer home in Karuizawa, in the Japanese Alps, as an escape from Tokyo's sticky summer heat. Dick coached the construction crew through the foreign process of building with logs, in a style dating back to pioneer days in Ethel's home state of Michigan.[70] This mode of building was also in vogue in the Adirondack Mountains of upstate New York, with many of Dick and Ethel's wealthy business associates.

Karuizawa Lodge formed a quadrangle, giving every room a view of an inner garden with a koi pond. Dick released budgies and canaries into the courtyard, which was netted over in summer. "My job was to fish out any young birds that fell into the pond because they weren't strong enough to fly yet," recalled Dick and Ethel's only surviving daughter, Marian.[71] A wide veranda overlooked the gardens, which were bounded by lava walls and a river Dick redirected to encircle the lodge, making their home an island unto itself. Ethel Andrews became an enthusiastic gardener, growing vegetables and flowers—a hobby she would later pursue on an even grander scale on Twin Islands.

The Andrews family flew the American flag and held an annual display of fireworks on American Independence Day. These signs of patriotism likely exacerbated their tenuous position in Japan, where Western influence remained unwelcome. In 1922, one of Dick's American stenographers was accosted on the street and accused of spying. And that fall Dick was arrested

---

69 Bill Andrews noted that his family began holidaying in Karuizawa in 1920, when they bought a four-hectare (ten-acre) property there.

70 Michigan is proud of its log cabin heritage and is the only state to celebrate an annual log cabin day, with festivals and tours. A massive log house near Ethel's hometown of Calumet was built at about the same time as the Karuizawa Lodge. The Calumet lodge is touted as the largest in the world.

71 *The Harrisons, 1890–1990.*

Dick and Ethel Andrews built a log home in the Japanese Alps, as an escape from the hot Tokyo summers. Its rustic style, popular among their peers in upstate New York, served as a reference for the foreman who oversaw the building of Twin Islands Lodge. *Charlie Rasmussen collection, courtesy of the Rita Rasmussen*

while boating with friends and family, charged with having taken photographs in a military zone.[72] "The origin of the whole thing was business jealousy,"[73] Dick told an English-language newspaper. The family's home and business office were ransacked, and cameras and pictures were seized.[74] But it was another two years before Dick was fined for the only indictable offence he'd committed: operating a boat without a licence. Ironically, a few decades later, he would again be suspected of spying, but this time as Japan's agent in Canada.

---

72   "Suspect American Photographed Fort," *New York Times*, October 7, 1922.

73   *Japan Times*, May 27, 1925, p. 2.

74   Marian said, in *The Harrisons, 1890–1990*, that her father was jailed for several days, but newspapers of the day say he was released immediately, out of respect for his business stature.

CHAPTER FOUR

Less than a year after Dick's arrest, on September 1, 1923, Japan was struck by an earthquake that measured 7.9 on the Richter scale. It was the noon hour, and many were cooking lunch over open flames that spilled over and set buildings alight—converging into fire storms and a flaming tornado. In the hard-hit Tokyo region, some of the victims died on the street when their feet got stuck in melting pavement. A tsunami followed, and 142,000 corpses were later pulled from the rubble of crushed and scorched buildings. An additional 40,000 remained missing. The Andrews family happened to be in Karuizawa at the time. Although they were 172 kilometres (107 miles) away, they saw towering flames rising above Tokyo. Dick's mother had remained in the city, so he hired a taxi to go to Tokyo. The streets were so clogged, he had to leave the taxi on the outskirts and continue on foot. He found his mother safe, but just as he approached his office, it burst into flames. His little dog Scotty dashed free just in time to be spared, though his tail was alight.

Andrews & George was a total loss,[75] including all their stock, which was collateral for an outstanding $1,000,000 loan (the equivalent of over $17,000,000 in 2022 currency). Rather than forfeit these funds, the bank extended its loan and Dick Andrews threw himself into a frenzy of rebuilding. Ethel's father (who now managed their New York office) came to Japan to help, but the gruelling schedule took its toll on Dick Andrews. "My grandfather had a nervous breakdown," says John Harrison, "[and] was nursed back to health by my grandmother in their log home in the mountains."

Dick rallied, and Andrews & George rose once again to success, through a rollercoaster economy that culminated in the stock market crash of 1929. But unlike America, where the Depression dragged on for a decade, prudent fiscal changes and increased military spending revived Japan's business sector by the mid-1930s. The government's rallying cry was "Enrich the Country, Strengthen the Armed Forces." And, as before, American steel brought in by companies like Andrews & George was crucial to militarization.

The Andrews formed a close friendship with Japan's royal family during these years. When there was to be a royal visit at their lodge in Karuizawa, even the long driveway had to be swept. "We would all sit on the porch

---

75 *The Harrisons, 1890–1990.*

Tonie Wong was an astute and savvy partner in the Andrews family's business affairs and a minor shareholder in the ownership of Twin Islands. Both she and Marian Andrews worked for US Intelligence Services during World War II. *Marian (Andrews) Harrison collection, courtesy John Harrison*

floor," recalled Marian. "[The prince would] sit on three pillows. His sisters sat on two. The rest of us sat on one or none." The Andrews family, in turn, visited the palace in Tokyo, where Marian joined the prince and princesses in their moated gardens while the adults played bridge. Foreign diplomats were invited to these bridge parties, including Dr. Hugh Keenleyside of BC, after he opened Canada's first embassy in Japan in 1929.[76] Both Keenleyside and the Japanese royal family would later prove pivotal friends.

By the mid-1930s, Andrews & George had 275 employees and offices in New York, Tokyo, Nagoya, Osaka, Saga and Hokkaido Island.[77] With a multi-million-dollar business, Dick Andrews had to keep a wary eye on international politics. He predicted a second global conflict early in the decade and feared his firm would get caught in crossfire with the Americans because Japan was openly allied with Nazi Germany. Some of their fellow expats, including their banker, left Japan, but the Andrews family hung on, seduced by a need to protect their fixed assets and take advantage of Japan's booming economy. They were in a precarious position. "The police arrested our cook, who had been with us for twenty years," recalled Marian. "They put him in jail [for two weeks] and grilled him about who came to our house." Her parents suspected their ever-changing roster of houseboys were government informers.

When Bill Andrews, who was ten years older than his sister, Marian, returned from college in the US in 1934, the family began to convert yen into foreign currencies.[78] It was a slow process because Japan had strict limitations on how much money could be removed from the country. Diplomat Hugh Keenleyside advised the Andrews to make BC their new home, assuring them Canadian tax laws were favourable.[79] "While I cannot remember the precise date," Bill Andrews later wrote, "it was just before the acquisition of Twin Islands that my father and Tonie Wong and I had a series of talks out of which grew a definite agreement."[80] Tonie persuaded friends working in various embassies to exchange wages paid in foreign currencies for yen at

---

76   Volume I, *Hammer the Golden Day, Memoirs of Hugh L. Keenleyside*, (Toronto: McClelland and Stewart, 1981) p. 265.

77   "Exporter Headed to Japan to Find His Lost Empire," *Vancouver Sun*, June 12, 1947, p. 11.

78   R.M. (Bill) Andrews's deposition, "Re the Estate of Richard Magill Andrews Deceased," courtesy Wendy Andrews.

79   "We felt, and still feel, that those accounts are no concern of any tax department in Canada," wrote R.M. (Bill) Andrews in personal reflections, courtesy Wendy Andrews.

80   R.M. (Bill) Andrews's personal papers, courtesy Wendy Andrews.

Dick and Ethel Andrews crossed the Pacific several times a year while Twin Islands Lodge was under construction, until the outbreak of World War II forced them to remain in BC permanently. *Marian (Andrews) Harrison collection, courtesy John Harrison*

CHAPTER FOUR

Andrews & George.[81] "[Miss Wong] was, in fact, instrumental in getting a large part of the necessary funds," Bill wrote. The family loaned this money to Maquinna Investments, a company they formed in BC, with shares held by Dick Andrews, Bill Andrews and Tonie Wong.[82]

Twin Islands was one of the company's first purchases.[83] "Dad always wanted to own an island," recalled Marian. There's an allure to the notion of an island, with its moat-like insularity, surrounded by the bounty and caprice of the sea. The Andrews family now had their own 281 hectare (694 acre) paradise. On Twin, they could fish, hunt and grow their own food, far removed from the chaos of a world once again headed for war.

Dick and Ethel spent increasing amounts of time in BC after this, though Japan was to remain their principal home for a few years to come. On each return visit to Canada, they brought more funds and personal effects. Some of their treasures—like Dick's wooden desk, with its silver roundels inscribed in Japanese script, his massive Irish wolfhound, and his old horse, Samu—were difficult to ship, but Tonie Wong made all things possible.

So began their gradual move, injecting millions of dollars into BC's struggling economy at a time when more than 30 percent of Canada's population was unemployed. The money the Andrews spent on land, housing, cars, offices, furnishings and business investments carried an exotic whiff of Asia—and raised questions about where their allegiances lay. "There were rumours of Japanese subs coming into the area, but this was never proven," wrote a Cortes Island resident, reminiscing about the Andrews family.[84] With no personal recollections from either Dick or Ethel, we're left

---

81   R.M. (Bill) Andrews's deposition, "Re the Estate of Richard Magill Andrews Deceased," courtesy Wendy Andrews.

82   Their shares in Maquinna Investments were at variable rates, as noted in R.M. (Bill) Andrews's personal papers, courtesy Wendy Andrews.

83   R.M. (Bill) Andrews's deposition of 1964, courtesy Wendy Andrews. The Andrews family purchased all five lots from the McCauleys on October 24, 1936, as noted in BC Lands Branch records. Twin was initially registered under Dick Andrews's name alone, but a decade later title was transferred to Maquinna Investments, to more accurately reflect shared ownership.

84   Charles Henry Pickles's family history, p. 10, Cortes Island Museum.

to speculate about what their views were, but circumstances suggest they sided with North Americans. When war was finally declared, two of their children became agents for US intelligence services in Washington, DC. And after the war, their son-in-law became an undercover spy based in Shanghai and Japan.

CHAPTER FIVE

Twin Islands Lodge

Twin Islands c. 1939, with the sprawling new lodge visible at the west end of Canoe Passage. *Marian (Andrews) Harrison collection, courtesy John Harrison*

Dick and Ethel Andrews saw Twin Islands for the first time in the winter of 1936.[85] The dense understorey of salal beneath cedar, spruce and Douglas

---

85 Marian (Andrews) Harrison thought her parents first visited Twin Islands for Christmas 1937, however foreman Charlie Rasmussen noted on his photos that work began

fir trees would have been dripping with trouser-soaking rain at that time of year. But, on a clear day, a climb to Twin's rocky heights presented spectacular views: a 360-degree panorama of the surrounding islands, the distant mountains on Vancouver Island, and the jagged peaks on the mainland, stark white against a blue sky.

Directly below were small farms and logging operations on nearby Cortes Island. The channel to the east was a busy shipping lane, with commercial fishing boats and tugs hauling log booms or towing straggling rafts of floating houses, steam donkeys and other equipment. Though the region was still sparsely populated during these Depression years, this was a busy working coast.

Twin was ideal in every way, with good fishing, astounding beauty, relative isolation—and proximity to the yachter's paradise of Desolation Sound. The well-developed homestead at its core was a bonus.

Dick and Ethel chose a building site for a lodge that winter. They wanted something reminiscent of their log home in Japan, at Karuizawa, and Twin had a ready supply of cedar. The rustic style they favoured had become increasingly popular among their wealthy American peers. The Vanderbilts, Astors, Guggenheims and Rockefellers all had summer homes built from logs in the Adirondack Mountains of upstate New York. Their homes were famous for their old-world craftsmanship, with features like fieldstone fireplaces and foundations, shingle roofs with broad overhangs, and hand-hewn twig furniture. Dick and Ethel wanted their lodge to be large enough to accommodate a dozen or more overnight guests, and it was to be winterized because it was going to be their principal residence.

The Andrews family hired Charlie Rasmussen[86] of Lund to oversee construction and brought him to Twin to see their chosen site: a rocky bluff at the northwest tip of the south island, at the entrance to Canoe Passage.

---

on the lodge in March 1937—so their first visit must have been Christmas 1936. See also *Powell River News*, September 17, 1952, for a reprint of an article first published in 1937 about the building of the lodge, courtesy Powell River Museum.

86 Charlie Rasmussen's daughter, Rita, thinks the McCauleys, who were former owners of Twin and close personal friends, likely recommended him for the job of foreman.

CHAPTER FIVE

Thirty-year-old Charlie Rasmussen had no previous experience in construction, but he proved the perfect choice to lead the team of craftsmen and tradesmen who built Twin Islands Lodge from 1937 to 1939. *Marian (Andrews) Harrison collection, courtesy John Harrison*

TWIN ISLANDS LODGE

"They laid out the plans, corner posts and stretched strings," recalled Marian. Dick Andrews gave Charlie Rasmussen two pictures of their lodge at Karuizawa and showed him how he wanted the logs notched. Shortly thereafter, he and Ethel returned to Japan, leaving Rasmussen to figure out the details.

Thirty-year-old Charlie Rasmussen was an interesting choice as their project foreman. He'd had plenty of experience with logging—which was to be his crew's first task—but he had minimal construction experience. It's likely that as a boy, he'd seen log homes being built, as this was the favoured building style among coastal settlers. Certainly, his elder brother Rick, who may have helped with the project at the outset, had some experience with log construction and went on to build a log airport terminal in the Yukon, which remains in use.[87] In any case, hiring an inexperienced foreman was a risky proposition, but as Jim Spilsbury of neighbouring Savary Island recalled, Dick Andrews was an astute judge of character. "He was a very trusting old man," wrote Spilsbury in his memoir.[88] "He'd meet you once, look you in the eye and either he would trust you or not. This young guy from Lund did a beautiful job." One of Charlie Rasmussen's many strengths was his ability to find experts for specialized tasks like wiring, plumbing, cabinetmaking, log work and masonry. And, as his son Gunnar recalls, the Depression made it easy to find both labourers and professionals. "There were a lot of men in need of work. People found Dad. Anybody who had experience just showed up."

Charlie Rasmussen's family had immigrated to BC from Denmark when he was a toddler, and he'd attended Lund's one-room school up to

---

87 Telephone conversation with Ed Rasmussen, youngest son of Rick Rasmussen, October 2022.

88 Howard White and Jim Spilsbury, *Spilsbury's Coast: Pioneer Years in the Wet West*, (Madeira Park: Harbour Publishing, 1987). Spilsbury appears to have confused the two brothers (Rick and Charlie Rasmussen), later recalling that Rick was the foreman. However, John D'Angio, a member of the lodge's construction crew, described the project in detail and said Charlie Rasmussen was the foreman. For the latter see: Bill Thompson, *Once Upon a Stump: Times and Tales of Powell River Pioneers*, (Powell River: Powell River Heritage Research Association, 1993).

the compulsory eighth grade. Thereafter, he worked in fishing, logging and trapping—doing whatever work was available in the lean years of the 1920s and the Great Depression that followed. His experience in logging (especially setting high rigging, a system of aerial cables used to pull logs from a cut-block to a loading area) gave him useful skills for the first phase of building Twin Islands Lodge.

Charlie hired most of his crew from among friends and relatives. Later in life, John D'Angio, an Italian immigrant with a homestead just north of Lund, reminisced about the project in a recorded interview.[89] "I went over to work for Charlie Rasmussen," recalled D'Angio. "He was building a big millionaire home on Twin Islands." D'Angio and a partner felled cedar trees on Twin, using a crosscut saw with a 2-metre-long (6.5 foot) blade that was dragged back and forth between two men. They cut 6,705 lineal metres (22,000 lineal feet) of cedar poles and purchased the rest from loggers on Cortes Island[90] and in Ramsay Arm,[91] north of Desolation Sound. They dragged the logs ashore with an old horse Charlie Rasmussen brought to the islands and debarked them on the beach using a long-handled tool called a spud, with a cupped, chisel-like blade.

Their next task was to build a causeway linking the two islands, which is thought to have been built during this early phase. Its function was not documented in early photographs, but a caretaker of later years speculates it allowed them to move logs cut on north Twin to the building site.[92]

Work began in March 1937, as Charlie Rasmussen's photographs show. They built a wide ramp up from Canoe Passage to the building site, using pulleys to drag logs and supplies into place.[93] The crew tested their skills and

---

89 Bill Thompson, *Once Upon a Stump: Times and Tales of Powell River Pioneers.*

90 Bruce Ellingsen of Cortes Island recalls that George and Wilf Freeman logged their Reef Point farm in 1937/8, selling some of the logs to the Andrews for Twin Islands Lodge.

91 Letter from Len Parker to Adrian (North) Redford, daughter of Alex North, the construction crew's head carpenter.

92 Jay Craddock, caretaker in the 1990s.

93 Rita Rasmussen's notes, taken from inscriptions on her father Charlie Rasmussen's photos of the building of Twin Islands Lodge.

Charlie Rasmussen (right) supervises the unloading of a five-ton barge load of materials for the construction of Twin Islands Lodge. *Marian (Andrews) Harrison collection, courtesy John Harrison*

design elements with small projects like kennels for Dick Andrews's 63-kilogram (140-pound) wolfhound (and a bitch and litter that soon followed), a generator shed and a two-bedroom caretaker's bungalow.

Fifteen or more people lived on-site during peak construction,[94] transforming the old homestead in Canoe Passage into a lively hamlet, where the crew was to live full-time for the two and a half years it took to complete the project. At least two of the men had families, including head carpenter Alex North,[95] whose wife, Aino, and infant daughter, Adrian, moved to the island with him.

The circumstances of their lives stood in sharp contrast to that of the Andrews family. Alex and Aino (Miettinen) North had both been born into Finnish immigrant families who'd had to work hard to forge new lives within a Depression-era economy. On a summer evening in 2018, I visited their daughter Adrian Redford, now 81, in her large home on a bluff in Finn Bay, near Lund. In the bay below, she pointed out the little blue house her

---

94 *Powell River News*, September 17, 1952, courtesy Powell River Museum.

95 Alex North's surname in Finnish was Pohjonen, which translates to "north."

CHAPTER FIVE

A few members of the construction crew stayed on after the Twin Islands Lodge was complete to work for the Andrews family. Head carpenter, Alex North (far left), stands beside construction foreman Charlie Rasmussen (now the Twin Islands caretaker and yacht skipper). To the right are Ralph Wenk (kneeling), his wife Eloise (sister to Ethel Andrews), Ethel Andrews, Dick Andrews and Cortes Island visitor Betty Jeffery. *Marian (Andrews) Harrison collection, courtesy John Harrison*

parents had built with their Twin Islands earnings. Adrian poured me a balloon-shaped glass of red wine, and her gleaming black cats crawled in and out of my purse as we chatted. She had fleeting memories of spending her first few years of life on Twin, making her the oldest living former resident.

Adrian is proud of what her parents achieved, given the rough economic circumstances of their early lives. As a young woman, her mother had worked in southeastern BC, cooking for a mine manager. While there, she met Alex North. After they were married in 1934, the couple got jobs as a cook and a butler in Vancouver, before joining Aino's family in Finn Bay. Alex was working away from home as a fisherman when Aino told him there was work on Twin. The job gave him an opportunity to use his self-taught woodworking skills, developed while building rowboats on the beach.

The Norths moved into an old scow propped on the beach below the homestead meadow in Canoe Passage in the early summer of 1937. The rest of the crew shared a bunkhouse on the west flank of the homestead

One of the crew's first projects was to build the caretaker's house, which allowed them to test log construction and design elements. *Marian (Andrews) Harrison collection, courtesy John Harrison*

meadow—"the farmhouse"—which was one of the first structures they built.[96] They also built sheds for chickens, ducks, goats, two horses, cows and pigs; a workshop; a smoke house, and a garage for a Fordson tractor. One man lived in a tidy little floathouse he dragged ashore on the site of Dan McDonald's former cabin. When the Andrews family visited, they likely stayed in James and Margaret Nixon's former bungalow on the east side of the meadow, though it was destroyed by fire at some point during these years.[97] Dick Andrews's Irish wolfhound romped among the busy crew and served as a pony-sized playmate for the children.

Several cooks took care of the crew's meals. Helge Goski, another first-generation Finn, was a lead cook. Like the Rasmussens and Norths, her family had also struggled to adapt during the Depression. She was born in a tent in a temporary camp at Comox, with only her father to assist with her birth. Helge had some prior experience before her move to Twin, having

---

96 This building remains on site but is now called "Pete's cabin."
97 Pictures show this house was still standing when the Andrews family first bought Twin Islands. Charred wood on site demonstrates it was razed, but there is no record of what happened.

CHAPTER FIVE

Helge Goski was the lead cook for the construction crew. She went on to marry Charlie Rasmussen, the construction foreman, and have two children while working on Twin. *Marian (Andrews) Harrison collection, courtesy John Harrison*

cooked for the Powell River Mill manager's family. Charlie Rasmussen valued this experience, but he appears to have had another motive for hiring Helge—they were married that same year and went on to raise their first two children on Twin.

Working on Twin wasn't easy. Initially the crew relied exclusively on hand tools because an electrical plant wasn't installed until a later phase. Both Helge Rasmussen and Aino North, who took in several crew members as boarders, required extra help because they had to haul buckets of water from the homestead well for cooking and cleaning. And with no telephone service available, Charlie Rasmussen brought in carrier pigeons to send messages back and forth to Lund.[98]

Three French-Canadians (whose names are no longer known) oversaw the log work, using a saddle-style of notching and shaping logs to interlock at the corner joins. "This type of log construction calls for much skilled axe work," said the *Powell River News* of 1937, "as all the logs are cupped together and calked, [for] the best joint possible."[99] The work was skillfully managed because the logs remain tight and straight over eighty years later. An engineer who stayed on the islands for a few months in the 1960s marvelled over the way modern conveniences like plumbing and wiring had been concealed within hollowed-out cavities in the logs.[100]

The crew lifted the logs into place using a spar tree rigged with lines and pulleys. Immense spans like the one in the palatial living room—which is more than 5,000 square feet—required an intricate meshwork of rafters to support the weight of its roof.

While the log walls were going up, John D'Angio and Charlie Rasmussen's father cut thirty cords of cedar shake blocks in Toba Inlet, to the northeast of Twin. "We cut the blocks six-feet-long and tumbled them into the river," said D'Angio. "We had a set of boomsticks that we put around them, and we coupled the boom to Old Rasmussen's boat and towed it to Twin. Then we cut and split all that stuff—the thirty cords—into shakes for the roof."

---

98   Family story, related by Rita Rasmussen in an email, 2018.
99   *Powell River News*, September 17, 1952, courtesy Powell River Museum.
100 Telephone interview with Captain Bill Mounce, 2019.

CHAPTER FIVE

Helge Rasmussen, lead cook, poses next to cedar shakes (roof shingles) split by hand for Twin Islands Lodge. *Charlie Rasmussen collection, courtesy Rita Rasmussen*

TWIN ISLANDS LODGE

Once the roof was on, the crew cleaned the log walls, which were then steamed inside and out, rubbed down with steel wool and painted with raw linseed oil.

John D'Angio also helped with masonry work, hauling rocks up from the beach for a stone fireplace that takes up much of the north wall of the spacious living room. "We lifted the big rocks with the horse and an A-frame," said D'Angio. Charlie Rasmussen was especially proud of this fireplace, later noting on one of his photographs that it was the lodge's masterpiece.

Rumours of the day suggested the lodge cost upwards of $50,000,[101] an astronomical sum at a time when the average five-room house in Vancouver sold for $1,200 to $1,600, while luxury homes fetched upwards of $4,000. The lodge's rambling footprint encompasses more than 10,000 square feet.[102] But rather than appearing as one sprawling building, its series of hip roofs made it look like a cluster of cottages. (Later, all these roofs were covered over by two overarching spans.) The two main structures, the bedroom

The Twin Islands Lodge took two and a half years to complete and is estimated to have cost $50, 000, at a time when luxury homes averaged $4,000. *Marian (Andrews) Harrison collection, courtesy John Harrison*

---

101   *Powell River News*, September 17, 1952, courtesy Powell River Museum.

102   John D'Angio said the lodge was 450 feet long, but a report in the *Powell River News*, September 17, 1952, said it was 260 feet long.

CHAPTER FIVE

Marian (Andrews) Harrison collection, courtesy John Harrison

Marian (Andrews) Harrison collection, courtesy John Harrison

wing and the living/dining room area, were joined by a 14-metre-long (45 feet) inclined hallway that follows the contour of the site. For reasons no longer known, Dick Andrews did not want any stairways inside the lodge, so the crew had to devise an inventive brace of interlocking logs to support this ramp. Four decades later, when Charlie Rasmussen revisited Twin, he was proud to find these joists had not buckled.

Dick and Ethel Andrews found it hard to visit BC in 1937 because Japan was at war with China. But they formed their Canadian company—Maquinna Investments—that year and started to seed it with loans. According to a Powell River newspaper, this is when Dick stocked Twin's marsh

Marian (Andrews) Harrison collection, courtesy John Harrison

The living room wing of Twin Islands Lodge under construction, with the roof going on, c. 1938. *Marian (Andrews) Harrison collection, courtesy John Harrison*

with exotic birds. "Mr. Andrews is interested in wild game and will have a variety with which to experiment. At present he has shipped from Japan, chukkers [a type of partridge common in India] and pheasants, [which he] hopes to see increase and thrive in this climate."

The crew built a 2.8-metre-long (9 foot) dam on the marsh in the summer of 1937 to block a stream flowing south into Echo Bay. Doing so

CHAPTER FIVE

redirected its flow into another creek running north through the homestead meadow, where they installed a Pelton wheel to generate electricity. This simple technology—generating hydro from a small, steady flow of water striking a spoon-shaped receptacle—remains popular for off-grid homes today. To ensure a constant supply during dry spells, they also installed three reservoirs as a backup.

It was also at this time—with the Andrews family unable to leave Japan to consult on the ongoing work on Twin—that the crew cleared a one-hectare (three-acre)[103] site near the marsh for a kitchen garden.

Dick and Ethel's return to BC for the summer of 1938 was announced with fanfare in provincial newspapers. Ethel, who arrived ahead of Dick,[104] directed the carpenters to make adjustments to the lodge's interior finishings.[105] She bought furniture, linens, dishes, vases and lamps from the Hudson's Bay Company store in Vancouver. She also arranged for their new yacht, *Twin Isles*, to be brought from Boeing's Vancouver shipyard to Victoria in readiness for Dick's arrival from Japan. Both Ethel and Marian were on hand in Victoria to wave Dick and his Irish wolfhound ashore from the *Empress of Asia*. This was the dog's third Pacific crossing in less than a year, said a newspaper. "He has his own private cabin aboard *Asia*, a former wireless room on the top deck, comfortably fitted out with straw bedding." From Victoria, the family travelled to Twin aboard their 14.5 metre (48 foot) yacht.[106]

Charlie Rasmussen tidied the meadow, beaches and building site before the Andrews family arrived. The lodge was now in the last stages of construction. The plumbing and wiring were complete, and two wood-fired steam heat furnaces were in operation, one beneath each of the two main

---

103 A 1950s sales flyer, courtesy Wendy Andrews, says there was a three-acre garden.
104 Travel documents, Wendy Andrews's family research.
105 Charlie Rasmussen told later owners, the Margrave and Margravine von Baden, that Ethel Andrews asked the crew to shift windows in the master bedroom to give Dick a great view from his desk.
106 *Colonist*, June 26 and 28, 1938. The boat was built by the Boeing Aircraft Company of Vancouver, BC and brought to Victoria by a Captain D. Johnson, in readiness for Dick Andrews's arrival from Japan.

wings. The lodge's new dock at the west end of Canoe Passage must have also been complete.

With a generator plant to augment their electricity supply, Dick Andrews bought radios for both the lodge and their new yacht.[107] Travelling radio salesman Jim Spilsbury installed and serviced the radios, in what was his largest sale to date. "I brought in the best RCA Victor sets, installed them, put up noise-free antennae, concealed all [the] wiring." His finale was a large radio set for the living room. It was the biggest set he'd ever built, and he was proud of the results. Dick Andrews had told him to spare no costs because he needed to remain in touch with his office in Tokyo. "It was one of the most elaborate stations on the coast and I was quite nervous about how it would work," recalled Spilsbury in his memoir. "When the job was finally done, [Dick Andrews] came in for the big test and handed me a number to call. It went through, and when the answer came it was from his son, Bill, in Tokyo. Then Andrews passed the handset over to me and said, 'Go ahead and talk!' I was speechless."

Work on Twin Islands Lodge culminated over the winter of 1938-39.[108] "The last job I did on Twin Islands was with Heimer Johnson," recalled John D'Angio. "We put 15,000 [square] feet of hemlock flooring in, and then we hand-scraped the whole thing—all the floors [with handheld glass blades]. Oh boy! We scraped for weeks, but it looked good after it was polished." Nearly eighty years later, the honey-coloured floors still gleam, and there is not a squeak in the 35-by-42-foot (10.6-by-12.8 metre) expanse.

Dick Andrews designed the lodge's furniture, all of which was built on-site by head carpenter Alex North, including tables, chairs, a chunky buffet, a cabinet, a 3.5-metre-long (12 foot) dining table, night tables, lounge

---

107 There is confusion about whether these radios were installed in 1937 or 1938, but as the Andrews family yacht was not launched until June 1938, it's likely they were installed after that date. A few decades later, on a return visit to the lodge, Spilsbury wrote in the guestbook that he first visited the lodge in 1937.

108 Marian (Andrews) Harrison said, in *The Harrisons, 1890–1990*, that the lodge was "largely complete by 1938," but photographs and some of the crew's recollections demonstrate work continued into the next year; and their real estate sales flyer gives the completion date as 1939.

CHAPTER FIVE

Construction foreman Charlie Rasmussen considered the large stone fireplace in the living room to be Twin Islands Lodge's masterpiece. *Marian (Andrews) Harrison collection, courtesy John Harrison*

Twin Islands Lodge's kitchen was a small room, by comparison to the vast L-shaped dining and living room, but it was backed by several store rooms. *Marian (Andrews) Harrison collection, courtesy John Harrison*

TWIN ISLANDS LODGE

The dining table was built on-site and was so large it could not later be removed from the building. The chairs, tables and bureau were also made for the lodge, using local wood. Dick Andrews commissioned a hand-painted dinnerware set in Japan, each piece depicting different North American birds. *Marian (Andrews) Harrison collection, courtesy John Harrison*

Marian (Andrews) Harrison collection, courtesy John Harrison

CHAPTER FIVE

chairs, bedsteads and bedroom bureaus. Much of it remains in use today. Alex North was a "real artist," recalled Len Parker, who joined the crew from his remote home near the head of Bute Inlet.[109]

Charlie and Helge Rasmussen were among the last to remain on-site, but Len Parker and John D'Angio also stayed to clear and plant the grounds. "[Andrews] wanted us to cut out all the stumps as close to the ground as we could," recalled D'Angio. "They were mostly big firs, around six- or seven-foot on the stump. For fifty cents a foot I cut those stumps off, knelt on the ground and cut them as close to the ground as I could. It would take about a day to cut a stump off, if you didn't hit a rock." This job alone took weeks, said D'Angio, who removed the bases of about 100 stumps. That done, the men planted dozens of exotic shrubs and roses imported from around the globe. Few have survived, though yellow-flowering laburnum later formed an invasive hedge in front of the lodge.

The crew also looked after the shellfish lease in Canoe Passage, where they seeded Japanese oysters.[110] Dick was fond of oysters and brought a barge load of several different kinds to BC. He wasn't confident they'd naturalize, so he set strict rules. They were not to be touched for several years, until they were well established and multiplying—which indeed they did. Descendants believe it was Dick Andrews who first introduced Japanese oysters into the region. They have since flourished to such an extent that oyster farming is now one of Cortes Island's primary industries.[111]

Flipping through her father's photographs of the building of Twin Islands Lodge, Charlie Rasmussen's daughter, Rita, is proud of his accomplishments. "Dad had so many different roles, from finding a crew, designing the layout around the existing topography, getting the required materials to the site, locating and logging all the cedar trees required, setting up a sawmill to process them—plus the use of a horse and all the hand

---

109 A letter from Len Parker to Adrian (North) Redford, recalling her father's work on the lodge.

110 BC Lands Branch records, registering a waterfront lease; and *The Harrisons, 1890–1990*.

111 *The Harrisons, 1890–1990*, claims Dick Andrews introduced Japanese oysters to the region, but others make a similar claim.

labour that went into the house," wrote Rita. The job taught Charlie Rasmussen cutting-edge skills like radio technology, plumbing, and heating and electrical systems, all of which were far beyond the scope of any other projects in the region at that time. The rest of the crew shared in his pride. Len Parker, the Bute Inlet homesteader, trapper and builder who would later have several volumes of poetry published, wrote an ode to the lodge.

Len Parker wrote a poem for the lodge, outlined in string and hung above the living room door. This photo shows the complex log joinery required by the lodge's many angles and levels. *Marian (Andrews) Harrison collection, courtesy John Harrison*

CHAPTER FIVE

Alex North outlined the words in string on a plaque that hung above a door in the living room, near the big fireplace:

> Quiet, where nature fondly smiles,
> Tempting as a mermaid's wiles.
> Peaceful view the soul beguiles.
> Home at last, sweet home, Twin Isles.

Twin Islands Lodge was complete by the summer of 1939,[112] but Dick and Ethel Andrews were not yet ready to make a permanent move to Canada. Their lives and work were still centred in Japan, though a global conflict was now clearly imminent. But they were determined to hang on until the last possible moment. They were in a dangerous position, especially after World War II was officially declared that September. Everyone knew that Japan was poised to enter the war as a German ally. If the Andrews family mistimed their final departure, their sizeable remaining assets in Japan, as well as their liberty—and their very lives—would be at risk.

---

112 A real estate flyer produced by the Andrews family, courtesy Wendy Andrews.

CHAPTER SIX

Living the Dream

The Andrews family owned a series of yachts, starting with the *Twin Isles* of 1938, which was conscripted for war service in 1940. *Marian (Andrews) Harrison collection, courtesy John Harrison*

With the launch of a swanky yacht, and the construction of a massive lodge on private islands, the Andrews family caused a stir in BC. They also bought luxury cars. When Dick Andrews showed up at a Vancouver dealership in his customary casual attire to look at Rolls Royces, he was ignored. But at a second car lot a salesman approached him immediately, so Dick bought both a Bentley and a Rolls Royce. Later, he returned to the first agency to

CHAPTER SIX

show them the results of good customer service.[113]

Such free spending stood in stark contrast to the grinding poverty most Canadians experienced in the late 1930s. While Japan's economy had rebounded by mid-decade, jobs remained scarce in Canada. Just weeks after Ethel Andrews had returned to BC in the spring of 1938 to prepare for her family's arrival, 1,200 unemployed men formed an angry mob outside the Vancouver Post Office, demanding relief assistance in a protest dubbed Bloody Sunday. Many were rounded up and sent to a makeshift work camp to fight a 30,000 hectare (75,000 acre) forest fire behind Campbell River.

Through the newest Andrews company, Maquinna Investments, they bought the Great West Salmon and Herring Cannery in Steveston, near Vancouver. They also wanted to buy a boat-building business, but that had to wait until they were living full-time in Canada. Meanwhile, they left the operation of Maquinna Investments in the hands of a Vancouver management firm.

On September 1, 1939, World War II was set in motion when Germany invaded Poland. Japan's support of Germany inflamed long-standing racism in North America. A friend of the Andrews family, diplomat Hugh Keenleyside, saw the rising tension first-hand when he escorted a Japanese prince and his wife across Canada a few years earlier. They were supposed to return via the US, but Keenleyside had to reroute the trip to avoid an angry mob in Washington State that was protesting shipments of American steel to Japan. The Longshore & Warehouse Union refused to load steel headed for plants like Andrews & George. (Coincidentally, among the demonstrators supporting the union was a young woman named Betsy Upper, whose son, Mark Torrance, would someday own Twin Islands.) "Hostility toward Japan was rising in Canada also," wrote Keenleyside in his autobiography, "as grim reports of the Japanese Army's vile behaviour in China continued to be received."[114]

Dick and Ethel Andrews returned to Japan that fall, despite the open risks. They'd moved out of their home in Tokyo earlier that year[115] and now

---

113 John Harrison, telephone interview, October 21, 2017.

114 Hugh Keenleyside, Volume I, *Hammer the Golden Day*.

115 *Japan Times*, June 6, 1939, p. 5.

lived in temporary quarters. Whether they visited Canada the following summer isn't known. This must have been an anxious year for them, hanging onto their business until the last possible moment, waiting for a signal to flee. It was Ethel's friend the Viscountess Momiji,[116] a Japanese noblewoman who'd been educated in Canada, who urged them to leave in the fall of 1940. Their final departure must have been especially difficult for Dick Andrews. It's easy to imagine him looking out his office window in Tokyo one last time, before turning over his keys to his staff. There was no way of knowing when—or if—he'd ever be able to return. But he'd prepared his staff for this eventuality, setting them up with a semi-autonomous business a few years before, under the name Daido Shoji K.K. Now his employees would take over the full operation.[117]

"He left everything there," wrote Jim Spilsbury. "He said there was no way around it, these military men were going to force this war, and he'd always known it."[118] Loss of assets weighed heavy on the Andrews family, after decades of hard work through good times and bad. Dick was leaving the place he considered home, says grandson John Harrison. "He loved Japan. It was really hard to leave."

On arrival in Vancouver that fall,[119] Dick and Ethel Andrews received a shock. "All the time he was in Japan," wrote Jim Spilsbury, "Andrews had been diverting his money to [their] agent, a prominent Vancouver lawyer,[120] to escape Japanese restrictions on foreigners taking money out of the country, but when he came to collect, the agent looked him in the eye and said, 'What money?' Andrews couldn't sue because what he was doing was illegal in an international sense."

Dick and Ethel Andrews, and Tonie Wong, rented adjoining apartments

---

116 *The Harrisons, 1890–1990*.
117 In Bill Andrews's deposition of 1964, he said his father formed Daido Shoji K.K. in about 1934, an employee-managed company handling the domestic market.
118 *Spilsbury's Coast*, pp. 133–34.
119 Bill Andrews said his parents left Japan in 1940, which is corroborated by a Powell River newspaper report. However, in *The Harrisons, 1890–1990*, p. 15, the year given was 1939.
120 Spilsbury did not give the name of the Andrews family's lawyer in *Spilsbury's Coast*.

CHAPTER SIX

Dick and Ethel Andrews (centre front) pose with staff at their import business headquarters in Japan. Dick Andrews was raised in Asia and considered Japan his home, so he was reluctant to leave, delaying his family's departure until after the onset of World War II. *R.M. Andrews III collection, courtesy Wendy Andrews*

in Vernon Manor, on the west side of Vancouver. Bill Andrews and his family soon followed, leaving Japan in January 1941. "Liner Full of Evacuees From Orient," ran a headline in the *Vancouver Sun*, announcing the last passenger ship to leave Japan for North America for years to come.[121]

Bill was dismayed to find his family's finances in turmoil, after several years of salting funds away in Maquinna Investments. He had to cover the costs of accommodation at the Hotel Vancouver on credit. "The expenses

---

121   There are differing accounts of the Andrews family's arrival. According to the *Vancouver Sun*, January 6, 1941, Dick Andrews Senior met his son, Bill, and family upon arrival aboard *Hiwawa Maru*. But ten days later the *Sun* of January 16, 1941, said both couples had just arrived from Japan. Bill Andrews later wrote in his memoirs, p. 7, that he and his wife and children left Tokyo in December 1940 and arrived in Canada in January 1941.

immediately began to pile up," he later wrote. "I checked with our investment firm and was told not to worry, that these were all being charged to my loan account." Shortly thereafter, the family severed ties with this firm, taking over the management of Maquinna Investments.

However dire this financial crisis may have seemed at the time,[122] the Andrews family had enough ready cash—or access to credit—to allow them to establish a second business, Magill Export Import Ltd.[123] This company soon had offices in Vancouver, Seattle, Manila, and Shanghai.[124]

A year after the Andrews family made their final move to Canada, on December 7, 1941, Japan bombed American naval ships in Hawaii's Pearl Harbour, killing over 2,000 Americans and injuring 1,200 more. Thereafter, the US joined active combat in Europe and in the Asia Pacific. North Americans of Japanese descent were stripped of their belongings and interned for the remainder of the war.

With their deep ties to Japan, the Andrews family now came under scrutiny. Dick Andrews had to certify that Tonie Wong did not have Japanese ancestry, to ensure her liberty. Jim Spilsbury recalled that a Canadian friend they'd met in Japan, who now worked for External Affairs in Ottawa, told Canadian intelligence services that Dick Andrews and his radiophone posed a threat. Dick must have seen the irony in this, with his arrest several decades before in Japan on suspicion of spying for the Americans. "They came up and confiscated all the fancy radio equipment I had built," wrote Spilsbury. He intervened, telling the authorities that phone service on Twin was routed through Vancouver, so it could not be used for covert messages. The battered equipment was returned for Spilsbury to reinstall.

Vancouver was now the business headquarters for Dick, Bill and Tonie Wong, but they spent parts of the year on Twin, joined by Marian on breaks from school. She loved the islands, hiking the trails and climbing north

---

122 Indeed, Maquinna Investments was to make substantial loans to Jim Spilsbury in the years ahead, when he started an aviation business. See Spilsbury Collection, University of BC Library, Special Collections, RBSC ARC 1517, Boxes 9-17.

123 BC historical directories, Vancouver Public Library, https://BCcd.vpl.ca/.

124 "Exporter Headed to Japan To Find His Lost Empire," *Vancouver Sun*, June 12, 1947, p. 11.

CHAPTER SIX

The Andrews family were all keen fishers, and the sport remained a lifelong passion for Marian. *Marian (Andrews) Harrison collection, courtesy John Harrison*

Twin's highest point, which the family called "Mount Marian." She brought friends home to enjoy her parents' warm hospitality and revelled in the region's terrific boating and fishing, which became her lifelong passions.

Charlie and Helge Rasmussen stayed on after the lodge was completed to serve as Twin's first caretakers. They were assisted by a fellow named Pete Banning, who took charge of the gardens, chickens, cows, and Dick and Ethel's old horse, Samu. It was a fluid transition. Banning had joined the lodge crew towards the end of their work, to plant and clear the grounds, moving into the farmhouse in the homestead meadow. The Rasmussens stayed on in the caretaker's bungalow, where they had been living for the past year.

The Rasmussens were ideal caretakers. Charlie Rasmussen knew the lodge and its infrastructure inside out. He looked after maintenance and monitored the massive radiotelephone, which had been moved into their bungalow, where it took up most of one wall in the living room. He was on standby at 6 p.m. nightly to pick up messages.[125] And when the Andrews family were in residence, he skippered their yacht—until it was conscripted for war service in 1940.[126] Helge (Goski) Rasmussen likely gave the lodge its annual spring cleaning and helped with food preparation, though the family had a full-time cook.[127]

There were sometimes as many as six youngsters on the island during the war years. The Rasmussens had two; Pete Banning's wife and two children stayed on Twin during school holidays;[128] and the two Andrews grandchildren were frequent visitors. It was a free and easy life, recalls the Rasmussens' son, Gunnar. The kids ran along the trail between the lodge and the homestead meadow amid a pack of dogs. They slid down the hay chute in the barn and tried to ride Dick Andrews's Irish wolfhounds. Like the fictional Darling family of *Peter Pan*, Gunnar Rasmussen had a large dog who watched over the children when they played on the beach. If they stepped into water higher than their waists, the dog herded them ashore.

The Rasmussen children weren't normally allowed in the lodge's living

---

125 Charlie and Helge's son, Gunnar Rasmussen, recalls that phone messages came through from Japan during the war years.

126 Nauticapedia website.

127 One of these cooks was Charlie Rasmussen's niece Edyth Hamilton.

128 Pete Banning's wife and children lived in Powell River during the school year, according to the *Powell River News*, courtesy Powell River Museum.

CHAPTER SIX

quarters, but when the Andrews grandchildren visited, they all played in the grand living room, with its wondrous mounted heads and big-game hides. On one such occasion, Ethel had filled some large glass vases with spring blossoms. Gunnar and the other children chased each other around the living room like puppies until something—his hair or shirt—caught one of the branches, and a vase went flying across the floor with a loud crash of broken glass, blossoms and spilled water.

The caretaker's job had many perks. The Rasmussens had speedboats at their command and a house with running water, a flush toilet and electricity—all of which were still luxuries in rural areas. But in about 1941,[129] Charlie Rasmussen turned in his notice. Gunnar had reached school-age, and Charlie was also concerned about leaving Helge on her own while he was off the island in winter for contract work.

Charlie had learned many advanced craftsmanship and technological skills and had a capacity for managing a crew, but he never again worked in construction. Finding a project of a similar scale would have required moving to an urban centre and leaving behind his extended family and friends. Instead, he went back to fishing and logging and ended his career clearing and maintaining hydro lines. His role in the building of the Twin Islands Lodge remained a proud highlight of his working life. "Dad loved to reminisce about Twin Islands," says his daughter, Rita, who was born after their move to Powell River. "It was part of our family lore—our psyche."

Head carpenter Alex North, along with his wife, Aino, and daughter, Adrian, followed as caretakers but, like the Rasmussens, they didn't stay long. Indeed, finding long-term caretakers would prove an ongoing challenge. Eventually the job fell to Pete Banning, who managed farm chores, lodge maintenance and security on his own. In winter, when Banning's children were in school in Powell River, he spent many weeks

---

129 The exact year is unclear. Charlie and Helge Rasmussen's son, Gunnar, thinks it was 1943 or 1944, but the Rasmussens' name does not appear in local directory listings after 1942. Dates on Alex North's photos suggest the Rasmussens left in 1942. Ted North (a grounds-crew man) said he took over answering the radiophone after Charlie Rasmussen left in about 1941. It's likely the truth lies in the middle, and they moved back and forth between Lund and Twin for a few years during this span.

Aino and Adrian North perched on one of the Andrews family's runabout boats, in 1939. When Charlie and Helge Rasmussen resigned as caretakers the Norths took over. *North family collection, courtesy Adrian (North) Redford*

at a stretch on his own, trapped by fog and foul weather. Windblown seas off Twin strike nearby Cortes and rebound in a backrush that makes boating risky. On a stormy day one fall, Banning was badly gored by a Jersey bull. He had to drag himself down to the shore, where he flagged down a tug that pushed through the backrush to come to his rescue, taking him to the Powell River Hospital.[130]

Banning's tasks were dictated by the seasons. In the quiet winter months, he made repairs and cleaned roofs and gutters. In spring, the garden had to be fertilized and planted, and the lodge had to be prepared for Dick and Ethel's return. "It takes Pete four days to vacuum-clean the main house," said a Powell River reporter, "which is a minor detail of his responsibilities, for he tends the engines, which include two tractors, a car, and a Fordson [tractor], power saws, generators, three motorboats, numerous other machines, the livestock and garden." In summer, when the Andrews family was in residence,

---

130 *Vancouver Sun*, October 21, 1947, p. 3.

CHAPTER SIX

Dick Andrews eventually had six Irish wolfhounds, weighing over 64 kilograms (140 pounds) apiece. The dogs each consumed about two and a half kilograms (six pounds) of dog food a day, so the Andrews had to barge in their food from Vancouver in bulk. Seen here is the caretaker's daughter, Adrian North, who is the oldest surviving Twin Islander. *North family collection, courtesy Adrian (North) Redford*

Banning delivered fresh milk, cream, eggs, fruit, flowers and vegetables to their kitchen door. Ethel assisted him with weeding, pruning and harvests. And one summer, when one of the wolfhounds bit off a cow's tail, Banning

LIVING THE DREAM

Ethel Andrews with one of Twin Islands' cows. Long-time caretaker Pete Banning took care of farm chores. When one of Dick Andrews's wolfhounds bit off a cow's tail, Banning made it an artificial replacement from a piece of hose and fraying rope. *Marian (Andrews) Harrison collection, courtesy John Harrison*

replaced it with rubber tubing, adding a swishy bit of rope at the end, so the animal could still swat flies. In the early fall, Banning helped Ethel preserve produce and the many fish her friends and family caught. One year alone, as Banning bragged to a Powell River reporter, Ethel canned 1,159 jars.[131]

Visits from Dick and Ethel's family became sporadic as the war years advanced. Their son, Bill, ran the Vancouver office managing Maquinna Investments. They secured at least one government contract for their shipyard, building a naval ship at a cost of $9,700. Their two daughters, Tonie Wong[132] and Marian Andrews, both got jobs with US Army intelligence in Washington, DC, in 1941, working as research analysts and translators. Marian assisted an engineer named Slim Harrison, who was drawing up plans to

---

131 "Enchanting Visit to Millionaire's Retreat," *Powell River News*, September 17, 1952, courtesy Powell River Museum.

132 According to Andrews descendant Jenny Young, from this point on the US would be Tonie Wong's home. Some years later she married Martin (Mert) Stone, a US naval officer she'd met in Japan. He retired as a Rear Admiral and the couple lived out their days in Orlando, Florida.

CHAPTER SIX

occupy Japan. She provided insider knowledge of Tokyo's largely uncharted streets and byways. "They assigned me to [the Japanese] Order of Battle, and I read captured documents," Marian later recalled. "I read the first captured document that came to the US. Our work consisted primarily of studying, analyzing and disseminating information about the Japanese Army." Her association with Slim Harrison soon led to romance, and they were married in 1945.

When the US dropped atomic bombs on Hiroshima and Nagasaki in August 1945, it precipitated the end of the war. Over 130,000 people died immediately, most of them civilians. Thousands more would suffer debilitating long-term effects. A month later, an armistice was signed, ending World War II.

Dick Andrews was among the first foreign businessmen to be granted re-entry into Japan in 1947. "Exporter Headed for Japan To Find His Lost Empire," ran a newspaper headline. According to John Harrison, Dick's grandson, he was shocked by the devastation he found there. "He walked through the rubble of destroyed streets and buildings. There was just one building still standing in the distance, so he walked towards it, never expecting his company's headquarters had survived—but it had." Dick's employees handed him back the keys and the family resumed their pre-war lives, commuting back and forth across the Pacific during the intense—but profitable—rebuilding of Japan.

"When Dad was allowed to return to Japan, he lost interest in Twin Islands," Marian recalled later. She pointed to ongoing problems over caretakers as a factor, but Dick and Ethel Andrews were now in their sixties, and dividing their energies between work and homes in both Japan and BC must have been taxing. In 1946, they advertised Twin Islands for sale in the *New York Times*, touting its many advantages, including 4,719 cubic metres (2,000,000 board feet) of timber (the equivalent of about 120 logging truckloads). The asking price was $137,000. This ad was picked up by the *Powell River News*, which ran it as a front-page story, but either the price was so steep it didn't sell, or Marian persuaded her parents to withdraw the property from the market—because it was another decade before they again put Twin Islands up for sale.

Among the post-war guests on Twin was the Viscount Alexander, a much-decorated World War II hero and the last aristocrat to be personally appointed by the British Crown as Canada's Governor General. He was so pleased with one of the many landscapes he painted during his month-long stay with the Andrews family that he entered it into a national exhibition in Montreal.[133] He and other visitors signed both the lodge's guest book, with its thick wooden cover incised with "Sweet Home Twin Isles," and a leatherbound fishing log. The latter was a record of catch sizes, species, lures and locales. Some added personal notes. "Fly was the creation of Ethel H. Andrews," wrote Marian's husband, Slim Harrison.

"A doggone dogfish chased the Spring on my hook to the top of the water—only quick action [from] Marian's netting saved my Spring for me," wrote another. General Sir Charles Loewen, a Canadian-born World War II hero who was now working for Britain, was among the last to sign this log. He had just been appointed commander-in-chief of the Far East Land Forces. Like everyone in the Andrews family, he was a keen sportsman, and later wrote a popular book on fly fishing.[134] Slim Harrison, Marian's husband and an undercover agent, had cultivated his friendship with Sir Charles based upon their shared passion for fishing, but in actuality his intent was to find out what Britain's intentions were in Asia.[135]

The lodge had a deserted feel when friends on a cruise from Washington State dropped by in 1952. The Andrews family were not in residence, but Pete Banning showed the visitors around. "This is a strange and lonely place," wrote John Ryan in the fishing log. "We stopped by with the Montgomerys—wanted them to see the house—anchored the *M.V. Mannana II* at the float. Pete was delighted to see us. He had lunch and dinner with us—and presented us with a crock of Twin Isles cream—Mary is watering flowers while I write this—there are lots of fish around & candle fish. Hope when & if we write in this log again it will be with the family present. Looks like this is it for '52."

With family visits growing less frequent, it must have been clear to Pete Banning that change was coming. The islands had been his home for over

---

133 *Nanaimo Daily News*, July 20, 1946, p. 1; and the *Gazette* (Montreal), March 21, 1947, p. 10. None of Alexander's paintings of Twin are represented in the collections of Canada's major galleries, nor are they featured in a published volume of Alexander's paintings.

134 Sir Charles Loewen, *Fly Fishing Flies* (Toronto: Pagurian Press, 1978).

135 *The Harrisons, 1890–1990*, p. 38.

CHAPTER SIX

fifteen years. He knew Twin's every nook and cranny: its seasonal moods, birds and plants—from the flowering dogwood trees of spring to the rattle of the wind and rain through the arbutus trees in fall. Banning's children were grown and gone, and his wife, Catherine, preferred to stay in Powell River. With so few visitors to the islands now, most of the apples in the homestead meadow fell to the ground in an aromatic heap. In the past those apples would have been juiced and sauced to fill gleaming jars in the root cellar. But now, the few that clung to the spiky branches were knocked free by varied thrush and enjoyed by Twin's many deer—Banning's steadfast companions.

In the spring of 1956, a boat arrived at the dock with Twin's new owners. Dick and Ethel Andrews had sold the property to two newspapermen, "much to my disgust," recalled Marian, who didn't speak to her father for half a year thereafter. Dick Andrews had largely retired by this time, suffering with cancer and heart disease. His son, Bill, managed the office in Japan,[136] and their Vancouver office was in the hands of a hired manager. On Christmas Eve in 1960, Dick Andrews died of pneumonia at the age of 75. Ethel Andrews outlived her husband by another twelve years, dying in 1972 at the age of 87. She lived long enough to see Twin Islands pass through various hands and its eventual sale to European royalty.

---

136 Bill Andrews's deposition of 1964, courtesy Wendy Andrews.

CHAPTER SEVEN
Turbulence

Hal Straight planned to selectively log Twin and build a destination resort, but a huge part of the islands' appeal for him was his love of fishing. He's seen here with his son Rob. *H.L. Straight estate*

Twin Islands was both an investment and a holiday retreat for its new owners: Hal Straight, the managing editor of the *Vancouver Sun*, and Max Bell, an Alberta oilman and publisher. Their initial idea was to selectively log both Twin and Hernando, which they'd bought a few

CHAPTER SEVEN

years before. Their plan was to develop Twin and Hernando into destination resorts.

Buying Twin was Hal Straight's brainchild, so he retained two of three shares in Twin Islands Lodge Limited,[137] a company he and Max Bell formed in 1956. His majority ownership, and closer proximity to the islands, made it logical for Hal Straight to serve as both property manager and company president. He was also the first to bring his family and friends there to stay, capturing their vacations on film.[138] Pete Banning appears in some of this footage, as a shuffling older man with a bent back. Unable or unwilling to adapt to all the changes, Banning soon gave notice and moved to Lund,

Every generation of Twin Islands children has played with the animal skins the Andrews family purchased to decorate the lodge, including Rob Straight. His father bought Twin in partnership with Alberta oilman Max Bell in 1956. *H.L. Straight estate*

---

137 Letter from Sutton, Braidwood, Morris & Hall, June 6, 1956, in Hal Straight's Twin Islands file, courtesy the Hal Straight estate.

138 Hal Straight's film footage, courtesy the Hal Straight estate.

where he lived out his few remaining years as a water-taxi driver.

The Straights travelled back and forth from Vancouver to Twin in a 5 metre (18 foot) wooden boat loaded with kids and fishing tackle. There's a chaotic tangle of lines, kids, dogs and adults in Hal Straight's footage, which later jumps to the arrival of a Pacific Western seaplane. Women in diaphanous skirts and large clip-on earrings unfold through a narrow aircraft door, followed by men in suits, ties and trench coats. Several frames later, some of these same people appear on the beach in bathing suits and shorts, or fishing in small boats. Among them is young Rob Straight in a striped shirt and jeans, his fishing gear and comic books clutched in hand. For this boy, summer on Twin was pure adventure, an experience he would later replicate for his own children on Hernando.

Hal Straight had first learned Twin was for sale through a friend, a young logger named Harry Castillou, who mentioned he was pulling together the financing to buy and log the islands. Hal suggested he and Max Bell make the purchase instead and hire Castillou to do the logging. But after the deal closed, Hal got cold feet about Castillou's relative inexperience and capacity to raise the necessary capital for a crew and equipment. He held firm to that position, though Castillou wrote a long letter of protest, outlining his skills and credentials. Castillou also said he was willing to stay on after the islands were logged to clear land for golf courses, swimming pools, landing strips and prefabricated cabins for a "tourist resort on a very high scale."[139]

But Hal Straight had to weigh his every move with care. Unlike Max Bell, who was a multi-millionaire, Hal had just started to branch out into property development and he was on the cusp of leaving his day job at the *Vancouver Sun*.[140] In an earlier conversation with Castillou, he'd compared himself in this career shift to a minor leaguer trying out for the major league.[141] The mortgage on Twin required him and Max Bell to repay the

---

139 In Max Bell's fonds, Glenbow Museum, M-6991-1205, there is a copy of a letter to Hal Straight from Harry Castillou dated April 23, 1956.

140 "Hal Straight of Vancouver Sun Resigns Post," Canadian Press article reprinted in *Nanaimo Daily News*, March 7, 1957, p. 1.

141 A short note penned across a letter dated March 24, 1961, in Hal Straight's Twin Islands file, suggests he and his partners had to compensate Castillou for the loss of a

financing within a year, but their plan was to use the proceeds from logging to accomplish this. For Hal, there was no room for missteps. Instead of hiring Castillou, he contracted with the more experienced B. and T. Logging to selectively cut 16,000 cubic metres (7,000,000 board feet) of timber, the equivalent of about 450 logging truckloads, on north and south Twin and on Hernando.[142]

Twin was to prove an astute investment, purchased on a low ebb in the real estate market. Where Dick and Ethel Andrews had asked $137,000[143] for Twin a decade before, they sold it to Hal Straight and Max Bell for $115,000.

It was changes to both the logging and fishing industries following the war that had caused property values to plummet on the Discovery Islands. All of the local canneries had relocated to urban centres by the late 1950s, and timber leases were being awarded to corporations instead of local operators. In addition, men and women who had lived and worked on location with their families in past decades now flew in and out of camps from larger centres like Campbell River. Indeed, it was the availability of seaplanes that brought about the greatest change, by edging the Union Steamship Company out of the freight and passenger business. Gone was the efficient and relatively affordable service Discovery Islanders had enjoyed since the 1890s.

Bob Langdon started the first seaplane business in the area in the 1940s, with a base in Campbell River. He was a daring 23-year-old pilot then and eager to find passengers, so he followed the Union Steamship Company's boats around the coast. He'd touch down wherever the ships docked to offer

---

"soft contract" to log, courtesy Hal Straight estate.

142 The amount of available timber said to be on the islands varies wildly in records of this time. The Andrews family's real estate flyer said there was about 2,000,000 feet (56,633 metres) and about 800 to 1,000 cedar poles on Twin. In Rob Castillou's April 23, 1956 letter proposing to log Twin, he said there was up to 72,000 metres of merchantable timber. He was not awarded the contract, according to *Nanaimo Daily News*, March 8, 1957, p. 3, which noted B. and T. Logging were working on Twin. In a March 24, 1961 letter in Max Bell's personal papers (Glenbow Museum), a man named Trouton was logging on Twin.

143 Hal Straight's Twin Islands file, with a handwritten note saying they purchased Twin for $115,000.

TURBULENCE

Vast economic change came to the Twin Islands region in the 1950s, when seaplanes replaced the Union Steamship Company. Seaplanes made it easy for distant owners to visit recreational properties. *H.L. Straight estate*

people rides to their final destinations in remote inlets. "The captain used to laugh at this funny-looking Seabee that used to follow him around," Langdon later recalled, "but he's unemployed now [and] we've got all the passengers."[144]

These localized economic problems were not reflected elsewhere in the province, where a post-war boom was facilitated by a pro-business government. As a newspaper man with his finger on the pulse of this time and place, Hal Straight saw opportunities galore. Just months after he bought Twin, he became the frontman for the development of Richmond Centre, which was to become one of the province's largest shopping malls.[145] And a year after he and Max Bell bought Twin, Hal Straight quit his job as managing editor of the *Vancouver Sun* to concentrate on property development.[146] He also began

---

144   Bob Langdon, tape-recorded interview, Museum at Campbell River Archives A59-1.
145   *Richmond Review*, November 14, 1956.
146   *Nanaimo Daily News*, March 7, 1957, p. 1; *Richmond Review*, March 13, 1957 and November 14, 1956, p. 1.

CHAPTER SEVEN

buying up weekly newspapers, including the *Campbell River Courier*.

But Twin Islands was more than just a good investment for Hal. It also appealed to his love of fishing and boating. His wife, Lottie, and their two children, Rob and Beverley, moved into the lodge that first summer, leaving Hal to commute back and forth to Vancouver. Lottie brought a stack of puzzles to occupy lazy afternoons and the kids made chocolate chip cookies with their housekeeper to fuel their explorations of the islands. They prowled through derelict barns and workshops in the homestead meadow in search of parts for metal sculptures, fished to their hearts' content, shot at tin cans and used the lodge's long, sloped hallway to the bedroom wing for movie screenings.

Hal Straight's files, photographs and films have been carefully maintained by his descendants. When I visited Hal's son, Rob, on a late summer afternoon in 2018, he and his daughter, Kelsey, were bent over an extraordinarily difficult jigsaw puzzle, scrutinizing pieces through a magnifying glass. Waves lapped against the embankment below their West Vancouver home. Kelsey showed me her recently self-published book, which delves into a young woman's life in Manhattan in a time of sexual, political and economic flux. Rob took me to his studio. He's made a name for himself as a commercial photographer and filmmaker. Like Dick and Ethel Andrews's descendants, here was another example of a multi-generational continuum of passions and predilections.

But while Hal Straight had shaped his son's future course, he was not an easy man to please. "I've got scars," Rob had told me on our first meeting a month earlier in Cortes Bay. He'd motored across from Hernando, where he and his wife have a seasonal home. Some of Hal Straight's colleagues also found his unlikely combination of gregarious charm and a sharp tongue a challenge. He was referred to among peers as the "fire-breathing" editor of the *Vancouver Sun*. Journalists who trained under Straight through the 1940s were left with mixed feelings. "Some despised him," wrote Pierre Berton later in life. "Some of his staff were terrified of him. His rivals hated him. But most admired him, and he was, in my opinion, not only the best managing editor in Vancouver, but also the best in Canada."

Jack Webster, who went on to become a combative media host, came to revile Hal Straight as his boss and mentor. "The day you die of [being] overweight, Straight, I'll be one of the ten thousand people who will dance on your coffin," Webster told him, in a clash over a rejected story.

"'You're fired,' screamed Hal.

'I quit,' bellowed Webster."[147]

As a young man, Hal Straight had been a trim athlete. A friend likened him to baseball star Babe Ruth, a comparison that must have pleased Hal because he'd started out in semi-pro baseball. But an injury had sidelined him, so Hal turned to sports reporting, which led to his job as managing editor. In the following years, he hit the scales at 113 kilograms (250 pounds), the impact of working in an industry with ceaseless deadlines and hard-nosed competition. "Both Straight and I were bottle-a-day men in those times," wrote Pierre Berton. "He hasn't had a drink for years now [but] he retains his gruff sense of humour. Hearing about the feats of one supposed two-fisted imbiber, Straight growled, 'Hell, I used to spill that much,'" recounted Berton.

Max Bell, Hal's business partner, had also started out in the newspaper industry. His father was the publisher of the *Calgary Albertan*, but when he died prematurely during the Depression, he left the newspaper in hock to a bank. Astute investments in oil eventually allowed Bell to bail the newspaper out and fulfill his boast to college friends that he'd one day be a millionaire. "His passion was business," recalls Max Bell's stepdaughter, Diane McMahon. "No matter where we went, he'd be on the phone, tracking investments and horse races." Even at social functions, says a contemporary, he'd be the life of the party one moment and the next he'd be off in some other room on the telephone.[148] "He would have loved this cellphone age," says McMahon.

Like Hal Straight, Max Bell was a man of contradictions: a calculating gambler who drove his Cadillac at devil-may-care speeds and a teetotaller who lived by a puritanical code. "The first thing he'd do every day was sit down to his breakfast of Hovis bread, bran flakes and skim milk to read the newspaper," recalls McMahon. "He never drank pop, coffee, tea or alcohol and spurned drugs of any kind." He was an "early-to-bed guy" with a

---

147 *Nanaimo Daily News*, November 2, 1990, from a review of Jack Webster's biography.

148 Captain Bill Mounce, November 17, 2018, telephone interview.

CHAPTER SEVEN

Helen and Bill Mounce, captain of Max Bell's 41 metre (135 foot) yacht *Campana*, seen here anchored off Twin Islands Lodge. Max Bell arranged cruises aboard his yacht for friends and associates like the Walt Disney family and Bing Crosby, with stops at Twin Islands. *Photo courtesy Shirley Whitehouse*

workout regimen, and a devout Presbyterian who kept his bible on his desk for daily readings.[149]

Diane McMahon remembers just one visit to Twin. She and her siblings left school early one Friday for a trip across the Rockies by train. In Vancouver, they boarded Max Bell's new 41 metre (135 foot) yacht, the *Campana* (which means bell, in Spanish), and motored up the coast to Twin, where the silent lodge struck her as a spooky, old-fashioned place.

While this is the only visit McMahon recalls, Max Bell made occasional stops on his own in the years that followed, tying up at the dock for a stay aboard his yacht. Max had a summer crew of seven for the *Campana*, including full-time captain Bill Mounce.[150] Max liked to treat friends and acquaintances like Walt Disney, Phil Harris, Bing Crosby and Canadian hockey star King Clancy to all-expenses-paid cruises on his yacht.[151] Celebrated writers

---

149 Earle Gray, *The Great Canadian Oil Patch: The Petroleum Era from Birth to Peak* (Calgary: June Warren Publishing, 2005), p. 189.
150 Captain Bill Mounce, November 17, 2018, telephone interview.
151 Captain Bill Mounce, email communication, May 2019.

were also among his guests, including Canada's Bruce Hutchison and Leland Stowe of New York, who wrote the enduring BC wilderness classic *Crusoe of Lonesome Lake*, in 1957. Stowe told Hal Straight he'd love to write his next novel at Dick Andrews's former desk in the lodge's master bedroom, but he never did.[152] Captain Mounce tailored the itinerary of each of these trips to the interests of Max's guests, often including stops on Hernando and Twin for picnics of barbecued seafood.

The demands of Hal Straight's career shift forced him to sell one of his Twin Islands shares within months to an associate of Max Bell's, Alberta oilman Cliff Walker. Bell and Walker had much in common. Both were self-made millionaires with large families, and both were deeply religious.

Though Hal Straight was no longer the majority shareholder, he continued as manager of Twin Islands Resort Limited. He printed stationery with Ulloa Lodge on the letterhead, inspired by the Spanish explorer's name for Twin. And he made on-site changes, like moving the dock from the west end of Canoe Passage to a small bay on the south side of the lodge. In the original configuration, the walk to the lodge was much shorter, but this change allowed Hal to build a saltwater swimming pool where the dock had been. His film footage shows a bulldozer pushing earth, likely taken from a bank on the north side of the passage,[153] down a slope in a cloud of dust to build a retaining wall for the pool. The wall didn't hold for more than a few summers, but it was fun while it lasted. Film footage shows family and guests lounging in deck chairs, watching leggy boys and little girls in floral bathing caps and frilly-bottomed swimsuits paddling in the shallow water.

Hal Straight sold his final share in Twin Islands to Cliff Walker within a year. "I might point out that it is with a sad heart that I am making this deal," he wrote to Cliff Walker, "as I think Twin Islands is the most wonderful spot of its type in this world and some day it will be of exceptional value." Though he no longer held a share, Hal continued as property manager,[154] but the

---

152   *A History of Twin Islands Lodge*, Hal Straight, courtesy his estate.
153   There is no record of exactly where the soil and rock were taken from, but 1990s caretaker Jay Craddock suggests it was excavated from the south shore of north Twin, in Canoe Passage.
154   In a letter dated December 27, 1957, Straight discusses the sale of his share to Walker,

CHAPTER SEVEN

arrangement quickly soured. A cursory note in his correspondence suggests there was a misunderstanding over the value of Twin's shares. "Walker found out Twin had been advertised for $125,000 & we only paid $115,000," Hal scrawled across a letter in his Twin Islands file. "He was sore, so wanted part of Hernando."[155] Cliff Walker told area merchants not to do business with Hal, but Max smoothed relations by buying one of Cliff Walker's shares, making Max Bell the dominant partner.

Caretakers managed the on-the-ground details on Twin throughout this time of changing ownership. Oscar and Hilda Fanning took over after Pete Banning left in 1956. They were sometimes joined by a widow named Veronica Dowling, who had a homestead in Tiber Bay on south Cortes. Dowling lived on her own and earned her keep as a farmer, a commercial fisher, a logger and a blacksmith. She had also trained to be a "ground observer," part of a Cold War defence system that relied on volunteers to keep a twenty-four-hour watch for enemy boats and aircraft. Twin was one of many ground posts scattered across the continent through the late 1950s, reporting to central checkpoints. Dowling's call sign, which presumably made use of Twin's radiophone equipment, was LIMA ECHO 9LEEMAH EKOHO ZERO ZERO BLUE.[156] Dowling was interviewed for a newspaper feature when this service was replaced by radar in 1960. She had forty scale aircraft models hanging from her ceiling as a reference, said the reporters, and she had made 17,777 marine and aircraft sightings during her six years as a ground observer.

There's no record of Dowling spotting enemy vessels, but her early warnings about forest fires and boats in distress were valuable. On one occasion, she heard a shouted call for help during the night and sent for Search and Rescue. She put a flashing light on her roof as a beacon for the victim, to signal help was coming, and the survivor was later plucked from the water near the entrance to Desolation Sound.

Twin Islands file, courtesy Hal Straight's estate.

155 Letter dated June 8, 1956, with a handwritten note in a corner, suggests Straight sold his share to Walker for its accrued value, courtesy Hal Straight's estate.

156 *Nanaimo Daily News,* January 13, 1959, p. 12. Veronica Dowling was stationed at the "Twin Islands Observation Post."

TURBULENCE

The growing intensity of the Cold War concerned many business leaders and politicians, who feared the threat of combat. Eager to explore diplomatic solutions, Max Bell hosted a bilateral US/Canada conference at Twin Islands Lodge. Delegates were to discuss cross-border trade and the role of the NATO alliance. Invitations were sent to dozens of businessmen, professors, oilmen, politicians, industrialists, media and union leaders through the winter of 1959. Twenty men signed on to spend three days at Max Bell's "log cabin resort" that September. Among them was Maine Congressman Frank Coffin, who presented a paper titled "The US Foreign Affairs Study of US-Canadian Relations." Canadian icon and former prime minister Lester B. Pearson, lauded for his leadership in de-escalating tension between the US and Cuba, was to speak to his paper titled "Our Common Problems."

Caretaker Oscar Fanning died suddenly just weeks before this conference, so Max hired a bright young German immigrant named George Lott to take over as caretaker for two weeks. Lott's wife, Shirley, looked after meals and housekeeping during the conference, with her 11-month-old baby in tow. She coordinated her efforts with the captains of Max's yacht and another boat, both of which provided additional accommodation. "We synchronized the meals," recalls Captain Bill Mounce, "so those staying in the lodge got the exact same food."

Shirley's busy schedule didn't allow her time to interact with the conference's distinguished guests, but Lester B. Pearson left a lasting impression. He slipped out to take a call, leaving a debate he'd found so thoroughly engaging he'd let cigarette ashes fall all over his jacket collar and lapels, giving this venerated Canadian leader a dishevelled appearance that seemed out of character.

Pearson wrapped up the conference with a rallying call for both countries to remain active within NATO. "If the hand-hewn log walls of Twin Islands Lodge were able, they'd tell some tall tales—and true—of the first Twin Islands conference," said follow-up media coverage. "I don't know at what intervals," Max Bell told the press, "but I expect we'll do this again." There were, however, few other reports about the conference to hint at its outcomes and insights. A columnist with the *Vancouver Sun* said the American attendees had been uncharacteristically quiet, and Lester B. Pearson urged Max Bell to invite some "tough-talking US congressmen" next time. But there was no second Twin Islands conference.

CHAPTER SEVEN

Pearson Speaks At Twin Isles

TWIN ISLES, B. C. (CP)—Greater participation by Canada in the North Atlantic Treaty Organization and in the defence of North America was urged by Liberal Leader Lester B. Pearson here Friday night.

Mr. Pearson, speaking at a Pacific conference on Canadian-United States relations sponsored by Calgary publisher Max Bell, also warned that the two North American members of NATO must take care that there is no rift with European members.

"I think it would be quite wrong if we didn't pay our share of collective defence," the federal Opposition leader told a dis- part in a way that is just as effective as a Continental part."

WARNING LINE COSTS
He made these suggestions:
1—Canada should take its share of the costs of the early warning line defences on Canadian soil even if they might be practical for only five or six years .
2. Canada should not prevent American forces from using Canadian facilities if arrangements for this use can be made which adequately p r o t e c t Canada's rights.
3. Canada should take a part to see that "backsliding" in support of NATO doesn't continue too far.

The growing intensity of the Cold War concerned business leaders and politicians who attended a bilateral US/Canadian conference at Twin Islands Lodge in 1959. *Nanaimo Daily News, September 1959*

"I don't think it gave him the satisfaction he expected," recalls Captain Mounce.

After the conference, George and Shirley Lott (now Whitehouse) stayed on as caretakers for six years. As Shirley recalls, it was Cliff Walker and his large family who made the greatest use of the islands thereafter—until they built a holiday home in Honolulu. Max Bell's focus likewise shifted after he purchased a 203-hectare (501-acre) ranch in Alberta, where he bred thoroughbred racehorses. With the islands again falling into disuse, caretakers George and Shirley Lott ran the lodge as a holiday rental for a season, advertising it with a colour brochure.[157] But the isolated location made it hard to find guests.

---

157 Colour brochure, Cortes Island Museum, Twin Islands vertical file.

In 1960, just a year after the joint Canadian/US conference, Max Bell and Cliff Walker asked Hal Straight to sell Twin. Hal wrote a short history of the islands and produced a flyer that caught the attention of an expat German forester and land agent named Henry Roethel. He was sourcing timberland in BC for German aristocrats who were shifting assets from Europe, fearing the Cold War would erupt into active warfare. Change—stirred up once again by global events—was poised to impact Twin Islands.

CHAPTER EIGHT

Fit for a Queen

Princess Anne, Queen Elizabeth II, and His Royal Highness the Duke of Edinburgh aboard the Royal Yacht *Britannia* in Vancouver Harbour in 1971. The yacht anchored off Twin, where the family stopped for a picnic on Mother's Day. *Bill Croke, courtesy of the Canadian Press*

The Cold War was a looming presence throughout the late 1950s and early 1960s. School children across North America dove beneath their desks to the wail of air-raid sirens, and some families dug underground shelters in their backyards. But North American anxiety was nothing compared to how

Central Europeans felt—many of whom had deep emotional scars from the last war. Some opted to emigrate to America. Others moved their investments offshore. Among the latter was Count Johann of Thun and Hohenstein, a young aristocrat from Czechoslovakia (now the Czech Republic).[158]

The count had moved to Austria after his country elected a Communist government in 1946. He was stripped of his ancestral properties, but his family had prepared for this eventuality by investing in large German corporations like Volkswagen.[159] In August 1961, the count married Grafin Theresia of Abensberg and Traun, and the couple honeymooned in BC. While there, they bought Twin Islands through a land agent named Henry Roethel. Hal Straight, acting as agent for Max Bell and Cliff Walker, scribbled a note across a letter in his Twin Islands file: "sold to the 'Volkswagen people.'"

The count had an almost immediate change of heart—or finances—because he sold the islands less than a year later to His Royal Highness Margrave Berthold of Baden, Germany. Henry Roethel again brokered the deal. When I interviewed the Margrave's grandson, Prince Bernhard, in 2018, he told me his grandfather, Berthold, sent his eldest son, Max, to Canada in search of property. They purchased Twin in 1962.

Prince Bernhard and I spoke by telephone. I was calling from the kitchen table of my 1890s log house on Quadra Island, and he was in his early eighteenth-century castle, which is really more like a small community. Its environs are big enough to include private quarters, a church, a public library and a boarding school.

Twin was a Cold War investment for the Margrave of Baden, whose title ranks above that of a count and dates to a time when Germany was a cluster of separate principalities. His wife, Her Imperial Highness the Margravine Theodora of Greece and Denmark, had experienced the tumult of World War II first-hand when her family was "chased around Europe,"

---

158 Little is known of the Count of Thun and Hohenstein, who has no direct descendants. Michael Joblokovski, a descendant of this royal line, provided what little details are known.

159 Shirley Lott (now Whitehouse), a caretaker of this time, recalls the count mentioning his investments in Volkswagen.

CHAPTER EIGHT

said her grandson, after losing their homes, properties, and much of their assets. Now, history seemed poised to repeat itself. Twin was to be an offshore investment and a safe haven in case of war. The idea of a pied-à-terre in America, says Prince Bernhard, had tremendous appeal to several generations of his family. "My grandfather loved hunting, and he was interested in forestry, which is an important part of the German economy," said the prince.

British Columbians were still caught up in anti-German sentiment, so there was public debate over millions of hectares of land being sold to German investors during the 1960s, but the sale of Twin was an exception. The "von Badens," as this family is known locally,[160] won immediate acceptance because Her Imperial Highness the Margravine Theodora was a sister to Prince Philip, consort to Britain's Queen Elizabeth II. "Royal-in-laws Buy Isle Close to Campbell River," ran a headline in Victoria's *Daily Colonist* newspaper in 1963.

The von Badens hired Campbell River pilot Bob Langdon to take them to Twin in his bulbous Seabee aircraft. "They're 'good Joes' who just want peace and quiet," he told a newspaper reporter. In proof of point, on the return flight Langdon called his wife from Campbell River to say he was bringing the Royal Family home for tea. Meeting intriguing coastal characters like Bob Langdon was to become a highlight of this family's tenure on Twin. Langdon was a local hero, admired for his many daredevil rescue flights. When a storm prevented Shirley and George Lott, Twin's caretakers, from getting medicine for their ailing son, Langdon braved the wind to drop a prescription at an agreed spot. Lott couldn't find the first drop, so Langdon made a second flight—this time with success.

Shirley remembers the von Badens fondly and has royalty scrapbooks dating back to her girlhood. The Margrave sometimes sat with her at the lodge's kitchen table to chat as she kneaded bread. Shirley became especially fond of the Margravine, who'd suffered a stroke. When Shirley saw her laboriously pecking out typewritten letters to Prince Philip, one finger at a

---

160 Titles are scrupulously maintained within German royalty, though the monarchy lost official status in 1918. The Margrave of Baden, Duchy of Baden, lives in southwestern Germany, bordering the Black Forest.

time, she offered to take dictation. "No," the Margravine told Shirley, "Philip knows how hard I have to work to write these letters and he appreciates them all the more for it."

After returning to Germany, the Margrave asked Shirley to source a book on North American birds and a pair of beaded moccasins for his wife. He died prematurely that same winter, at the age of 57. The Margravine lived on for another six years, but never returned to Twin Islands.

Title to Twin passed to their eldest son, His Royal Highness Maximilian (Max) of Baden. He and his brother and other family members made occasional summer visits, but after his marriage to Archduchess Valerie of Austria in 1966, the islands became their annual retreat. On a visit in 1971, they invited Bob Langdon and his wife, Jackie, to lunch at the lodge. "The

The British Royal Family's visit to British Columbia in 1971 caused a sensation. Seen here, a crowd awaits their arrival in Victoria. BC Archives 61925

CHAPTER EIGHT

young Margravine was a lovely, fun person," recalls Jackie.

During BC's centenary celebrations in 1971—marking the province's entry into Canadian confederation—news flashed through the media that Queen Elizabeth, Prince Philip and their daughter, Anne, would cruise the coast in the Royal Yacht *Britannia*. Stops were planned at Powell River for a Mother's Day church service, followed by a picnic on Twin. Organizers anguished over details like whether to pass the church's collection plate to the Royal Family (the answer was yes). Security was scrutinized in both locales, and a special stairway was built to accommodate the *Britannia*'s launch, which was too large for Twin's dock.

The 126 metre (413 foot) *Britannia* anchored off Powell River on a pristine blue-sky day, and thousands cheered the Royal Family ashore. "The three were in a friendly, smiling mood as they stopped to speak to individuals," wrote a reporter with the *Edmonton Journal*. Two hundred and twenty-five people packed the town's little Anglican church. All eyes were trained on the Queen, who wore a violet-coloured wool jacket and a pleated skirt, topped by a pale mauve cloche hat. The Royal Family joined in hymn singing, and Prince Philip read aloud from a new bible purchased for the occasion.

The von Badens were not yet in residence, but their new caretakers, Julie and Del Neal, welcomed the royals to Twin. The Queen's staff spread a picnic beneath a flowering dogwood tree and prepared a barbecue on the beach. Later, the Neals opened the lodge and invited the Queen to sign the official guestbook. "And mine too," said Julie Neal, thrusting forward her personal guestbook, a possession that remains a treasure. The royal visit ended with a stroll through the grounds and gardens.

The von Badens and their four children—Princess Marie-Louise, and Princes Bernhard, Leopold and Michael—arrived some weeks later for their annual six-week stay. "Living on the BC coast was really my father's dream," recalls Prince Bernhard. "He identified with the mountains, trees and wilderness of this rugged coastal setting." Like his father before him, His Royal Highness Max von Baden was also fascinated by local residents. He looked up Charlie Rasmussen, the construction foreman who'd built Twin Islands Lodge. Charlie and his wife, Helge, took the von Badens to the Powell River A&W drive-in restaurant in their big blue Chrysler. "It could accommodate at least three or four in the front seat and squeeze five in the back," recalls the

Rasmussens' daughter, Rita, remembering the days before seatbelts were mandatory. "Dad would always pay the bill as a treat for everyone in the car." The A&W carhop brought burgers, chips, onion rings and thick glass mugs of root beer on a tray that was clipped to the car's window. "Enjoy yourselves," said Charlie Rasmussen. "The meal is on me."

The von Badens sometimes rented a yacht to explore further afield, going to places like Bute Inlet to see some of the highest peaks in the province. They visited logger-trapper Len Parker, who'd been a member of the lodge's construction crew and had composed the poem hanging above the entrance to the living room. Several books of Parker's poetry had since been published, and his editor, Laurette, had become his third wife. Laurette's coiffed hair and painted nails seemed out of place in the wilds of Bute Inlet, but the couple had struck a satisfactory compromise, dividing their time between the inlet and Victoria. Parker is remembered by many as a gifted storyteller, which made him a favourite guest at Twin Islands Lodge. Stories of Parker's youth as a prairie cowboy and his encounters with the grizzlies, wolves, raging rivers and glaciers of Bute Inlet so captivated Prince Bernhard, as he told me in our telephone interview, that they later became bedtime favourites for his own children. "Can you tell me a story, Papa?" was usually answered with one of Len Parker's tales.

The von Baden home in Germany dates back centuries, but the family was nonetheless charmed by the history of Twin's lodge. They gave explicit instructions to their various caretakers not to change a thing, from the furniture and décor, to displays of hand-painted dinnerware that Dick Andrews had commissioned in Japan. "It was like going back in time," recalls Prince Bernhard. In the evening, after the generators were turned off, the family lit flickering oil lamps, and the children played with the lodge's antique bedroom telephones, which served as an internal intercom system.

Twin was an escape from worldly cares for the von Badens. Sometimes, they received as few as one or two telephone calls during their whole stay. When the sea was warm, the Margravine loved to swim, especially at night, diving through sparkling phosphorescence. "My mother mentioned the peace, the freedom, the countryside and the comfortable lodge," wrote Prince Bernhard in a follow-up to our phone conversation.

Regardless of who owned the lodge, the caretakers' jobs remained much the same. Their duties included maintenance of the buildings, boats, dock

CHAPTER EIGHT

Their Royal Highnesses Max and Valerie von Baden (left), with their two eldest children, Princess Marie-Louise and Prince Bernhard (squatting) in Twin Islands Lodge. Their guests, at right, are Niki von Brucke, Prince Ludwig von Baden, and Princess Marianne von Baden. HRH *Max von Baden collection, courtesy Prince Bernhard*

and the kitchen garden. Since upgrades and renovations were rare during the von Badens' time, the off-season was more relaxed. But when the family was in residence, full housekeeping services were required. "It was an incredibly big household to manage," recalls Lella Gmeiner, a caretaker in the 1980s, "with their four young children, a nanny and frequent guests." Gmeiner and a helper made a different dish for every meal, using fresh local ingredients. "The food available to us was fantastic," says Gmeiner. She and her husband, Bernie Anderson, and their daughter, Noba, raised chickens, caught crabs and fish, and grew a wide variety of vegetables, fruits and berries.

The von Badens sometimes formed random friendships, like the time they met Bob Lacey of Powell River on the beach. He shared a salmon barbecue, cooked in the manner of the Tla'amin people, and the Royal Family was so impressed Lacey became an annual summer visitor. He has fond memories of hiking Twin's park-like trails through a mixed forest of widely spaced Douglas fir, cedar and hemlock and a noble stand of giant broad-leafed maples in a grove above Echo Bay. One tree had a remarkable 3-metre-wide (almost 10 feet across) burl. "The islands were exceptionally beautiful," says Lacey. All the grasses and underbrush were kept trim by Twin's deer, many of them so tame that Lacey was able to run a finger along the fuzzy nap of a buck's antlers in velvet.

The children of the various caretakers and their helpers were playmates for the Royal Family. Bernie Anderson built the kids go-carts to whiz down the dirt trail of the sloping homestead meadow; and, one summer, he helped them erect a zipline above the beach at the dock. On Sundays, everyone on Twin came together for a shared meal at the lodge's long dining table.

Henry Roethel remained the property manager for much of the von Baden years, paying the bills and overseeing forestry. Upon hiring new caretakers, he instructed them to address the von Badens as "His Royal Highness" and "Her Imperial Royal Highness," but it was hard for children to keep these titles straight. One youngster came up with his own inventive adaptation, calling them "Momma and Poppa Highness." Lella Gmeiner and Bernie Anderson followed proper protocols in their first year as caretakers—but, when the von Badens returned the next summer, Gmeiner thrust out her hand and welcomed the Margrave as "Max." "His jaw dropped," recalls Gmeiner, "but after the initial shock, he accepted it."

Paul and Magdalene Knepperges of Lund took over as caretakers in 1989. Marian (Andrews) Harrison paid a return visit to Twin during their time. Her parents—Dick and Ethel Andrews—were long since dead, but Marian wanted to see how the islands had fared. She was surprised to find how little had changed in the lodge. "Everything was exactly the way I remembered it—rugs, furniture, everything. It was eerie."[161] Even the knitted bedcovers her mother had made for every room were still in use.

The lives of the caretakers swung from the busy social scene of summer to the isolation of winter, when southeast storms kept them island-bound for weeks at a stretch. Some caretakers found the long winters depressing. Others were surprised by their ability to adapt. The von Badens' second caretakers, Del and Julie Neal, had accepted the job because it was Del's dream to live on a remote island. His wife, Julie, was pleased to find Twin's isolation suited her, too. Paul and Magdalene Knepperges, who'd grown up

---

161   *The Harrisons, 1890–1990*, p. 18.

CHAPTER EIGHT

surrounded by friends and family in a tight-knit village in Germany, had also come to the islands because it was Paul's dream to live in the BC wilderness. Like Julie Neal, Magdalene found life on the islands was a perfect fit. She and Paul learned to garden and came to know and love the local birds, plants and animals. "I never felt lonely," recalls Magdalene. "I would still be there, if [the von Badens] hadn't sold."

A highlight of their decade on Twin was a three-day visit by Queen Elizabeth and Prince Philip in 1994. They got their first clue something unusual was afoot when an airplane buzzed close overhead that winter. The Kneppergeses happened to be on the lodge's roof at the time, removing fir needles and debris. One low fly-over was odd, but the plane returned for another close-range pass. The next day a police boat hovered just off the dock, with cameras flashing, and shortly thereafter the Kneppergeses learned Queen Elizabeth II and family would visit Twin that summer. Canadian and British security services combed the islands and a scuba diver checked beneath the dock, presumably searching for explosives. The two servant bedrooms off the kitchen were turned over to top officials from Canadian and British security services, but these arrangements had to be altered when it came to light that one of them was terrified of rodents.[162]

Hospitality plans came under scrutiny, too. The Queen's "advance protocol staff" suggested the von Badens get rid of the old scatter carpets Dick Andrews had commissioned for the lodge in the late 1930s, and they also wanted to hire a professional chef, but the Margrave refused on both scores. No changes were to be made to the lodge, and he was confident Magdalene Kneppergeses would do a splendid job of cooking for the Queen. This was just as well, as Magdalene recalls, because a professional chef would have balked at the lodge's small, antiquated kitchen, with its Depression-era appliances.

Magdalene hired two women to help with advance cleaning, food prep and housekeeping during the royal visit. One of them was Ginnie Ellingsen, a Cortes Islander and a British immigrant. She kept a scrapbook as a memento of her brush with royalty. It included the instruction sheet she and the others received with protocols from Buckingham Palace: "It is appropriate for ladies to make a half curtsy, i.e. the right foot is placed

---

162 *Vancouver Sun*, August 22, 1994, p. 1.

Caretaker Paul Knepperges meets her Royal Highness Queen Elizabeth II at Twin's dock, on arrival for her three-day visit in July 1994. Standing behind them are Prince Leopold and HRH Max, Margrave of Baden. *Ginnie Ellingsen estate, courtesy Bruce Ellingsen*

behind the left heel, the knee bent slightly, and the head is held erect as the presentee shakes hands with the Queen and the Duke of Edinburgh." The serving staff were to address the Queen as "Your Majesty" on first introduction and later as "Ma'am." For Prince Philip, it was "Your Majesty" on first introduction and thereafter "Sir." The Royal Family didn't eat fish when they were away from home, so the team bought local chickens and lamb, and harvested fresh produce from Twin's lush garden (though doing so required clearance from the security crew circulating around the islands with sniffer dogs). Meals were to be laid out buffet-style, leaving the Queen to the care of her personal maid. "It was all very exciting and dramatic!" recalled Ginnie Ellingsen, in an interview.

Upon arrival, the von Badens and their two youngest sons, Princes Leopold and Michael, lined up with their staff to welcome the British Royal Family at the dock. Queen Elizabeth removed her gloves to shake hands, said Ellingsen. One glance into "those kind, wise eyes" impressed her with a realization that this woman, a figurehead for millions of people around the world, was just a "small, gentle woman."

CHAPTER EIGHT

The Royal Family were adaptable guests. When Magdalene Knepperges noticed the Queen's maid was making repeated trips to the kitchen for kettles of hot water, she discovered the pilot light had blown out on the bedroom wing's hot water tank. Rather than complain, the maid was making do.

There were no official announcements of the Queen's visit, but most locals knew of her stay. George Sirk of Cortes hatched a scheme to have his wife, opera singer Kim Paulley, serenade Her Majesty with "God Save the Queen" early one morning. Ten friends joined them, rowing a boat across to Long Tom Island, a bald cluster of rocks off northwest Twin, just within a no-go zone patrolled by the RCMP. The police stopped Sirk's and Paulley's crew as they were about to land. "We're just going to sing to the Queen," they said. The police conferred and allowed them to continue. After all, recalls Sirk, how much harm could a group in a rowboat do at such a distance?

Kim Paulley followed "God Save the Queen" with "Summertime." Her powerful voice carried over the water on a northwest breeze, captured on film by professional videographer Bill Weaver. The crew ate their early-morning breakfast of muffins, coffee and tea and rowed back home to Cortes. Sirk hopes the Queen heard Kim Paulley's lovely serenade. But if not, she must have learned of it that evening, when Weaver's footage aired on national television.

Queen Elizabeth II departs Twin Islands aboard a floatplane after a three-day stay that included a serenade at dawn by local opera singer Kim Paulley. *Ginnie Ellingsen estate, courtesy Bruce Ellingsen*

Queen Elizabeth II had looked tired on first arrival on Twin, taxed by her many official duties for the opening of the Commonwealth Games in Victoria. On departure, she looked rested and refreshed, recalls Magdalene Knepperges. Her three-day stay became Twin's moment of glory. While many of the larger, populated communities on the Discovery Islands remain relatively unknown, a mention of Twin Islands draws a smile of recognition for its association with Queen Elizabeth II.

Of the four von Baden children, only two had been on hand to welcome Queen Elizabeth and the Duke of Edinburgh that summer. All were now in their teens and embarking on their adult lives—a hint that Twin's time-capsule years were drawing to a close.

CHAPTER NINE

The White Knight

Mike Jenks and Peter Shields cut 33,000 cubic metres of red cedar and Douglas fir on south Twin within months, a volume that would have taken three decades to log under the von Badens' forest management plan. A flotilla of protesters drew attention to the impact this logging would have upon the fragile ecology of a relatively small island. *Iris Steigemann*

When family holidays became difficult for the von Badens to arrange in the mid-1990s, they told their caretakers—Paul and Magdalene Knepperges— they might sell Twin Islands. The Cold War was over, so the need to maintain offshore investments had passed. And though selective logging on Twin helped pay its expenses, a slump in Germany's economy had put a strain on the family's finances, forcing them to sell one of their six castles.

THE WHITE KNIGHT

The Kneppergeses braced themselves for change, but nothing transpired in the months—and then years—that followed. No prospective buyers came around. Nor did the Kneppergeses see any real estate listings. So, when Twin's property manager showed up in the summer of 1997 to say the von Badens had just accepted an offer from BC logger and developer Mike Jenks, they were shocked.[163]

This was the worst possible scenario, from the perspective of the Kneppergeses. Mike Jenks was portrayed in the media as a destructive clear-cut logger who converted forest land into multi-lot developments. He was embroiled at the time in controversy over logging various coastal properties, including 1,760 hectares (4,349 acres) to the south on Denman Island, with a lush wetland at its core. The Kneppergeses wrote to the von Badens to express their concern, but they were swamped with business at home and left the matter with their lawyer and their current property manager, KPMG of Vancouver.

Jenks had only seen Twin from afar before making his offer, so completion was subject to an on-site assessment of timber values. Bobo Fraser and Judith Williams, summer residents of Refuge Cove (near Desolation Sound), happened to be showing a relative the lodge the day Mike Jenks and some associates arrived. Judith later described Jenks as "an unpromising-looking fellow," in his ripped T-shirt and jeans. She engaged one of his associates in a "snoopy exchange." "He looked kind of stunned and said, 'We had no idea this big house was here!'"[164] This did not bode well for the preservation of what Judith, a visual artist and coastal historian, viewed as one of the region's premier heritage sites.

Questions still linger for the Kneppergeses, Judith Williams, and Bobo Fraser about how Jenks came to learn the von Badens might be willing to sell. But making unsolicited offers such as this is common practice for this logger and property developer.

---

163   The late Peter Shields, owner of Coastland Wood Industries and Shields Navigation, is not often mentioned in recollections of this sale because he was a silent partner.

164   Mike Jenks knew about the lodge, which was listed among Twin's assets, but his friend appears to have not known about it. Telephone interview with Mike Jenks, November 2, 2018.

CHAPTER NINE

Mike Jenks operates within a specialized niche. Unlike multinational logging corporations, who must follow stringent regulations on long-term Crown leases, logging private land is loosely regulated. The downside for Jenks's style of operation is the need for large, upfront capital. And another factor Jenks must weigh is that many of the properties available for purchase are located in populated areas, so he often faces protests. (Perhaps this explains why his partner in this deal, Peter Shields, opted to take a backseat role.) But on the upside, minimal regulations and the option to later subdivide the land can bring ample returns. "That's my business," Jenks told a newspaper reporter a few months after he bought Twin, when controversy erupted over logging the islands. "I find property with enough timber to make it worthwhile. I buy it. I log it and develop the land. It's what I do."[165]

As Mike Jenks recalls, he started out by approaching the von Badens' lawyer in Victoria to discuss buying Twin. The lawyer conferred with the property manager, KPMG, and a deal was struck. "They set the price, and we agreed to it," Jenks told me.

When word spread among locals that Mike Jenks had bought Twin, several people wrote the von Badens to let them know their agreed price was below market value. At this, the Margrave consulted with George Reifel, a Vancouver businessman and real estate agent. George was surprised not to have been contacted earlier. He owns a share in neighbouring Hernando Island and has decades of experience in the high-end real estate market, specializing in private islands and waterfront properties. KPMG had often asked his advice about incidentals like fuel sources and caretakers, but no one had thought to ask for his input as a real estate agent. Someone in the mix was "either stupid or crooked," quipped another coastal realtor, who still puzzles over the speedy sale of Twin.[166]

George Reifel arranged for the von Badens to meet with one of the best lawyers in the province to see if the deal could be rescinded, but it was too late. The offer was ironclad. The best George could do was help pack

---

165 Vancouver *Province*, February 22, 1998.
166 Interview with Bobo Fraser and Judith Williams, June 7, 2018. See also *Ecological Assessment of Twin Island*, in which a consultant noted the von Badens' agent had "perhaps not acted in their best interests."

the family's personal belongings in readiness to turn Twin over to its new owners. The sale closed on December 1, 1997, at $4 million,[167] a price Mike Jenks still contends was fair for both parties. As he recalls, he paid about half this per hectare value just months later for a large property north of Victoria.[168] But a more comparable sale was that of Jedediah Island, south of Powell River, which is about 20 hectares (50 acres) smaller than Twin. It sold two years earlier at $4.2 million, which was $2.3 million less than its appraised value—a concession made by the owners, who wanted Jedediah to become a provincial park.[169]

The Kneppergeses were fearful of what lay ahead for Twin, but Mike Jenks assured them his plan was to selectively log, taking only about 30 to 50 percent of the total tree cover. He wanted to maintain a parklike setting for a subdivision of about thirty recreational waterfront parcels. Each 2-hectare (5-acre) lot was to include a share in large tracts at the core of both islands, along with communal ownership of the lodge and its dock.

A crew of about eight loggers started work just days after the deal closed. When Paul and Magdalene Knepperges visited the first cut-block, they were outraged. From their perspective, compared to the low-impact selective logging of the von Baden years, this was a scene of utter devastation. The loggers were leaving just a few sensitive areas, like a remarkable stand of maples and a fringe of perimeter trees. "Wherever there were sufficient trees to log," recalls Magdalene, "they took everything."

Jay Craddock, whose family had logged on Twin for the von Badens, recalls it differently. Jenks's crew "hit hard and fast," acknowledges Jay, but this is standard practice in an industry with high daily operating costs. "I've seen worse clear-cut logging," he added.

The Kneppergeses gave immediate notice and were gone within days. Many Cortes Islanders were also shocked by the extent of the logging on

---

167 Mike Jenks said in a telephone interview in November 2018 that he bought Twin Islands for $4.4 million, but the purchase agreement (courtesy George Reifel) shows the price was $4 million.

168 This forested acreage on the Malahat was yet another property owned by German royalty, who purchased it during the Cold War years.

169 *Nanaimo Times*, March 4, 1995, p. 6.

CHAPTER NINE

The protest against logging on south Twin was aimed at new owners Mike Jenks, his silent partner Peter Shields, and their bank. *Iris Steigemann*

south Twin. A loosely aligned group—many with properties overlooking Twin and a few who'd formerly worked for the von Badens—banded together to take action. Iris Steigemann's home on south Cortes became their meeting place. She'd worked for many years as an assistant housekeeper on Twin. Protestor Bernie Anderson also had a personal connection, having once been a caretaker for the von Badens. "I'm dedicated to stopping this," Anderson told a reporter, who covered their protest. Anderson said Twin was one of the most beautiful places in Georgia Strait. "They're prying the jewel out of the crown. I am furious. I am livid."

Realtor Martha Abelson, who lives on south Cortes, documented the protest in an online journal. She said Jenks's crew had stripped about 3 hectares (7 acres) of fir and cedar trees within the first week. Eleven heavy machines were due to arrive in the new year to pile blasted rock along the shore to stabilize it for loading logs onto barges. The machines were also used to haul logs, reshaping a stream that flows from a marsh into Echo Bay.

The protestors asked to meet with Jenks, armed with negative examples of what clear-cut logging can do to the fragile ecology of islands. Marina Island, to the west, had been stripped of its trees in the 1980s and regrowth remained painfully slow three decades later. (A local logger says it'll be a century or more before Marina regains a healthy mixed stand.)[170] A similar story had also played out to the northwest of Twin, on Read Island, where heavy machinery exposed broken rock throughout a large cut-block. What remained was a poor medium for regrowth.

People associated with Hollyhock Leadership Learning Centre, an education centre that overlooks Twin, were also concerned. "Hollyhock was birthed by Greenpeace founders," says Joel Solomon, whose leadership role with Hollyhock dates back many years. "Environmental concerns are deeply embedded in this organization's values," says Solomon.

Mike Jenks agreed to meet with concerned residents, but a lack of shared values made it impossible to find a compromise. Jenks pointed out that he was creating jobs. His crew was staying at a local motel and using the Klahoose Band's water taxi service—until escalating antagonism forced him to find services elsewhere. And his subdivision would create short-term local employment when building sites were developed. But these arguments fell flat. While most Discovery Islanders of the first half of the twentieth century had made a living as loggers, only a handful now did. The protestors wanted the logging stopped, or at least scaled back. While whole hillsides were being clear-cut far from sight in the region's remote inlets, this logging was taking place on the opposition's doorstep—and they were ready to fight.

Jenks remains puzzled to this day by the disconnect between his values and those of residents. "My philosophy," he told a reporter at the time, "is 'why are you so against this? Don't you want your kids to have a place to live?'" He maintains this position today, wondering what gives people who cut trees on their own properties and live in wooden houses the right to protest logging.

When talks with Mike Jenks failed in February 1998, about sixty protestors took to the water in small boats with banners flying. They got assistance from the Sierra Legal Defence Fund to pay for ads, taking their campaign public in hopes of shaming Jenks into negotiation—but instead it reinforced his resolve. "They're not going to stop me," Jenks told a reporter for *The Province*. "If anything, it will make me more determined."[171]

---

170   Gerry Cote.
171   Vancouver *Province*, February 1998.

CHAPTER NINE

But while this battle raged on, a behind-the-scenes solution was being negotiated. Carol Newell, a relatively new Cortes Islander and a partner in the Hollyhock education centre, felt something had to be done to save Twin. Carol was moved to act by her love of nature and an unusual dream she'd had the summer before. In it, she saw an eagle lying on the shore at the water's edge. The bird appeared to be dying. On approaching it, she found it was injured and—in a perplexing act of self-destruction—it was pecking at its own wound. It was shortly after she'd had this dream that Carol first heard rumours that Twin had been sold to a logger. She was now resolved to stop him, and she had the means to do so.

Carol Newell had established a foundation called Endswell a few years before Twin was sold to Mike Jenks, and it was now managed by Joel Solomon.[172] She asked Joel, as well as her accountant and her lawyer, to find a way to save Twin. "We need to stop this," said Carol, "even if it means buying it. Get together and find a way." Joel Solomon was concerned about how much capital this would remove from Endswell, which was serving a growing number of organizations. But Carol says she was determined, even though this was not her usual style. "We need to make this happen," she told Joel, who approached George Reifel to act as their agent.

George Reifel was pleased to accept. He was a seasonal resident of Hernando and a proactive third-generation conservationist,[173] whose brush with cancer in his mid-twenties had lent urgency to his commitment to preserve wilderness areas like Twin for future generations. Unbeknownst to George at the time, he was stepping into what would evolve into a lifelong stewardship of the islands.

Joel Solomon told George Reifel to offer Jenks and Shields $1 million above what they'd paid just a few months before. This seemed generous to George, but Jenks and Shields did not want to sell. Twin was a long-term

---

172 Newell later created Renewal Partners, which invests in ecologically and socially responsible businesses.

173 Reifel considers himself to be a "conservationist," preserving and utilizing land without harming the natural environment. As a long-standing volunteer with Nature Trust of BC, Reifel has helped secure high-profile properties like the 4,047-hectare (10,000-acre) Hoodoos Ranch in East Kootenay. The vendor was Mike Jenks.

Carol Newell, then a partner in the Hollyhock Leadership Learning Centre on Cortes, was inspired by her love of nature to organize a deal to save Twin Islands from logging. *Courtesy of Carol Newell*

investment for them, and to this day Mike Jenks still feels the subdivision they had in mind would have been "one of the most unique recreational properties on the coast."

Carol Newell refused to take no for an answer. "We need to just buy it," she told Joel Solomon. Logging was underway and talk of barge-loads of

CHAPTER NINE

logs leaving Twin fuelled her drive to see it stopped. "Not only was an intact island habitat being decimated," Carol recalled two decades later, "but we had just revitalized Hollyhock, where wild country is celebrated, only for it to have a view of utter devastation."

Her team's plan was to place restrictive covenants on Twin, limiting both logging and the number of allowable building sites, before reselling. Carol's resolve was steadfast, and bargaining continued until an agreed price of $10 million was reached in March 1998. Chainsaws and grapple yarders ground to a halt as Jenks and Shields stepped back from a project that netted them a fast return of $6 million in land value, plus several million more in logging. They'd cut 33,000 cubic metres (1,165,384 cubic feet) of red cedar and Douglas fir on south Twin.[174] Under the von Baden forest management plan, it would have taken about three decades to cut a comparable volume.[175]

From Mike Jenks's perspective, an offer from an anonymous buyer involved risk, but George Reifel assured him the purchaser was "highly qualified"—though George himself did not yet know who the actual buyer was. He was relying on Joel Solomon's good name. And Mike Jenks was, in turn, relying on George Reifel's integrity. "We basically did the whole deal on almost just a handshake," recalls Jenks.

In 2018, I met with Joel Solomon on Cortes Island. His cliffside property overlooks north Twin and is backed by the broad expanse of John and Margaret Manson's former farm. "Hippies use this door," says a sign at one of his entrances. Joel, who exudes confidence and financial savvy, gave me a fast-paced overview of Carol Newell's philanthropy, which has funded an impressive list of community initiatives on Cortes and elsewhere. "Carol is a quiet heroine of accomplishments far beyond what even she recognizes, inspiring others to follow her lead," Joel told me. Carol's foundation was the largest of its kind in the province at that time, he added,

---

174   *Ecological Assessment of Twin Islands*, p. 5, notes the cut was 33,000 cubic metres, though Mike Jenks's recollection is he cut about 20,000 cubic metres. The protest group speculated Jenks and Shields cut 40,000 cubic metres.

175   *Ecological Assessment of Twin Islands*, pp. 2 and 5. Appendix A notes the von Badens' annual cut was 1,700 cubic metres per year, which aligns with the calculation of a planned cut spread over 35 years.

making significant contributions to endangered wilderness areas like the Great Bear Rain Forest.

Later that same day, I visited Carol at her home on a bluff near Mansons Landing Park. She met me in her front garden in bare feet and a layered summer dress. Her eyes lit up as she talked about the extravagantly coloured and tentacled creatures she's encountered while scuba diving, the seasonal arrival of ducks in the bay outside her home, and the many eagles and other birds that nest on Twin.

Carol laughed over the memory of a clandestine visit to Twin Islands after her offer had been accepted. She wore bulky clothing and a big hat to keep from being recognized by caretakers or their guests. Hiding her identity as a wealthy philanthropist was then imperative, allowing Carol to maintain friendships and associations on an equal footing. "I don't identify with my wealth," she said. Keeping her affairs private also kept her from being the object of unsolicited pitches for funding.

By 2018, when I interviewed her, Carol Newell was no longer a behind-the-scenes benefactor. She'd stepped out of the shadows to take a leadership role among her peers, urging them to join her in supporting what she describes in presentations as "community and ecological wellbeing."

But back in March 1998, when Carol Newell's foundation bought Twin, she still maintained anonymity, leaving area residents and visitors to puzzle over the identity of the "white knight" who had saved Twin.

Quiet once again reigned on Twin. Southeast winds swept the tides over Echo Bay's scarred shore. The laburnums burst into soft yellow bloom in front of the lodge. And eight pairs of eagles reared their young in their enormous nests, refurbished year after year atop Twin's remaining old-growth Douglas fir trees.

CHAPTER TEN

Contemplating Eternity

Mark and Susan Torrance standing in front of their new greenhouse, 2002. *Courtesy Mark Torrance*

Jay and Sonia Craddock followed the Kneppergeses as caretakers in the summer of 1998. They had no idea who owned the islands, but George Reifel—now in the dual role of real estate agent and property manager—was in charge. They helped install two new furnaces and hot water heaters and kept the place safe and tidy. In hindsight—compared to the decade that followed—they remember that summer as a relaxed idyll.

Living on Twin was a perfect fit for the Craddocks. Jay, who grew up on the Discovery Islands, had worked with his father's crew when they selectively logged on Twin for the von Badens. At thirty, Jay was still in the early stages of his working life, earning most of his keep as a log salvager and commercial fisherman. His experience with boats, tides, southeast storms and the maintenance of temperamental mechanical systems were assets. Sonia liked living close to the land and sea, and she enjoyed learning to garden on a large scale and to handle boats in all kinds of weather.

Meanwhile, Carol Newell's team talked through the details of restrictive covenants, setting parameters for future logging, and limiting the number, size and location of house sites. The covenants were to apply to both islands, though Carol decided early on not to sell north Twin, at least for the time being. "I felt I was a steward of the island, holding it—lightly," she recalls, "because it's a place that belongs to itself."

Carol's protective instinct toward north Twin grew that summer, when she invited close friends to join her in a "vision fast." She and twelve others spent four days and nights on the island, each in their own sequestered spot, with just a tarp, drinking water, warm clothing and a sleeping bag. On arrival, they congregated on a low-lying northwest peninsula and hiked a bluff which brought them in view of an eagle's nest in the upper branches of an old-growth Douglas fir. Two gawky eaglets crouched among sticks and feathers, "with faces only a mother could love," recalls Carol, whose dream about an eagle the summer before had made a lasting impression on her.

The vision fast experience is transformative, says Carol. "After days of silence and not eating, you really drop down into the land. Everything slows down, and the moments become increasingly meaningful. It's a time for review and introspection and inviting a new vision of how to live life purposefully."

At this same time, Carol's team was drafting restrictive covenants for Twin. Once these were in place, George Reifel listed south Twin for sale. A couple who'd made a fortune in Seattle's tech industry were interested, but in mid-process the man was diagnosed with a terminal illness and had to step aside. Others followed, but their values—assessed through Endswell's job application style process—weren't a good match. The asking price, restrictive covenants and the need to provide personal details made selling Twin a challenge. Joel Solomon, George Reifel and some friends visited the islands at this time. "If you are able to find a buyer that will accept the covenants," one of Joel's guests told George, "we will buy you a case of Chateau Lafite."

CHAPTER TEN

Mark Torrance, who holidayed in Desolation Sound from boyhood, wanted to buy property in close proximity to this yachters' paradise. The jagged peak of Mount Denman is seen here in the centre backdrop. *Jeanette Taylor*

That same summer, another area realtor, Bobo Fraser, showed local properties to another couple from Seattle: Mark Torrance and his fiancée, Susan Summers. "We hired him to find a small place, maybe five acres, in Desolation Sound," recalls Mark Torrance. "A place we could tie up the sailboat and possibly build a cabin." But none of the few listings available met their requirements.

Mark had a deep attachment to this part of the coast, with its fjords, uninhabited islands and snow-capped peaks. He'd spent many summers here, starting when he was a boy of seven, sailing to Desolation Sound with his pal Joe Golberg and family. Later, as young men, they each bought small boats and sailed in tandem to the Sound. "The power of the wind and moving many tons of boat quietly through the water was thrilling," recalls Mark. Later, when he was a young married man with children, Desolation Sound became a favourite holiday destination.

In 1999, when he was 53, Mark was on the cusp of marrying once again— and he wanted his fiancée to see Desolation Sound. Susan was immediately captivated. Real estate agent Bobo Fraser had little to offer them within the park's environs, but he suggested they look at Twin Islands. "He said it may be available at some point, but I wanted a place in Desolation Sound, and I thought Twin was too far west," wrote Mark, in recollections of this time. "We continued our search through the summer, but Bobo kept saying, 'Just look at Twin.'"

On a return trip that September, Mark and Susan finally acted on Bobo Fraser's advice. "It was a sunny, crisp, beautiful day in the middle of September," wrote Mark. "During the twenty-minute trip, the grandeur of Desolation Sound captivated us." George Reifel must have coached caretakers Jay and Sonia Craddock well, recalls Mark. They'd baked fresh bread and had a fire ablaze in the massive stone fireplace. Twin Islands Lodge both looked and smelled heavenly. "I'll never forget arriving at the dock and seeing the lodge and caretaker's cottage for the first time," wrote Mark. "We walked up this beautiful long path that wraps the south end of the bay and into the lodge. The place was amazing. I'd never seen anything like it. It was straight out of the 1930s and gorgeous; completely furnished. The smell of bread and cedar logs was unforgettable. Susan and I were hooked from the moment we stepped onto Twin."

"We quickly decided to purchase Twin and began dreaming about the possibilities," wrote Mark. "We didn't know the friendships we were about to form. We had no idea how Twin would transform us, our friends and our visitors. We didn't know where this adventure would lead and how it would challenge us."

The initial tour skirted the logged-over areas on south Twin, so the muddy devastation of clear-cutting was not apparent, recalls Mark. The unusually strong windstorms that were to follow over the next few winters had not yet toppled what few trees Jenks and Shields had left standing in the centre of the island. Mark and Susan walked a beaten path overhung by fir, maples, alder and arbutus, up the hill through the old homestead meadow, past a barn, the farmhouse and outbuildings to see the big garden and orchard near the marsh. On a return visit with Endswell's agent, George Reifel, the couple's enthusiasm grew. "You could tell Susan, in particular, was so excited about the place," recalls George. "Especially the garden." It had long been Susan's dream to have a large garden, and here was the opportunity.

Mark Torrance had just stepped away from a high-flying business career

CHAPTER TEN

and he was ready for a new challenge. "I had equity and liquidity, which was simply a bunch of digits on a computer," he recalls. Purchasing land in a beautiful natural setting, with its lovely smells, trees, tides and warm water, had huge appeal.

But the couple's first flush of excitement in this serendipitous find quickly transformed into an emotional rollercoaster. For starters, Mark found Endswell's application process invasive. "I've never been interviewed and scrutinized to buy something before," he recalled in an interview in 2018. "But I kept quiet and plodded through the paces because I was so interested in Twin." That done, lawyers on both sides haggled over the complexities of Endswell's restrictive covenants. Few lawyers had experience with covenants at the time, so Mark's Canadian attorney had to research every step. To make matters more challenging, his lawyer fell under Twin's spell, says Mark, sometimes advocating for more restrictions, instead of fewer.

Miscommunication caused delays, too. "Several times we thought we had an understanding [but] the documents would reflect something else," recalls Mark. "The seller's approach [to the covenants] was to nail down everything in fine detail." Building sites were limited to eight, in addition to the existing housing, and none could be within sight of south Cortes or Hernando. Every detail of construction was specified, including size, outdoor lighting, siding colours and roofing materials. There were to be no bright lights on Twin, no commuting helicopters, no landing strips, no jet skis, no generators on boats after sundown and no long-term guests living on boats, to name a few of the provisos in a thirty-three-page document.

With talks dragging on, relations became fraught. Caretakers Jay and Sonia Craddock were on hand for a heated exchange between Mark and his lawyer. "I was not always patient," remembers Mark. He and his lawyer later came to realize there were significant differences in American and Canadian styles of negotiation. In hindsight, Mark feels they should have worked harder from the outset to bridge this culture gap. The Craddocks were surprised by Mark's blunt negotiating style and decided if the deal closed, they wouldn't stay on as caretakers. "He was showing his muscle in those negotiations," recalls Jay Craddock now.

But the Craddocks got glimmers of a softer side of Mark's personality on visits that followed. Though the sale had not yet closed, George Reifel gave Mark and Susan permission to bring friends and family to the lodge for the American Thanksgiving weekend. It was this visit that cemented the couple's deep attachment to Twin. "In the chilly evening, a huge fire in the living room fireplace radiated warmth and the kids ran up and down the long hall," wrote Mark. "A large black-bear rug came alive when Susan put it on like a cape, its head over hers, and chased the kids around the living room." On another occasion the Craddocks helped Mark and Susan plant spring bulbs, even though there was not yet any assurance they'd ever enjoy the blooms.

When talks stalled that winter, with Endswell's lawyers proving inflexible on some key points, Mark's lawyer told them the deal was off. As Mark saw it, there was no point agreeing to provisos he knew he couldn't meet. One of several sticking points was oversight of the covenants. Typically, they're managed in perpetuity by an arms-length organization certified by government as a covenant holder. Mark feared the prospect of negotiating specifics with a slow-moving board of directors. But just as he had resigned himself to losing this opportunity, Endswell's lawyers agreed to an individual covenant holder, and George Reifel accepted this role, becoming one of the few individuals to be certified as such by the provincial government.[176]

Mark and Susan were in Mexico when they finally got word the sale was ready to finalize. Joel Solomon of Endswell was also away, on a retreat on the Ganges River in Varanasi, where communication was difficult. He had to sort through the final terms over a crackling telephone line at 3 a.m. India time. Mark and Susan, meanwhile, flew home and were in George Reifel's Vancouver office to sign off on the purchase on Valentine's Day, 2000. They were ecstatic. On their first visit as owners, they invited Jay and Sonia Craddock to remain as caretakers. Having come to know Mark and Susan better, the Craddocks agreed to a ninety-day trial. They were curious about what lay ahead.

In the weeks and months that followed, the two couples forged lasting bonds over shared meals and endless discussions, bouncing ideas back and forth about renovations and improvements to south Twin's buildings and infrastructure. Ideas were captured on scraps of paper during lunch

---

176   Having earned both Endswell's and the Torrances' trust, Reifel negotiated the finalization of the restrictive covenants for both north and south Twin.

CHAPTER TEN

breaks, as they tackled their first project: expanding and planting the garden. There was limited equipment available, so one of their first purchases was a rototiller.

"We had no idea what we were in for," recalls Mark. "No idea how complicated it would be to own and operate Twin; no idea of the joy and challenges." But those were insights gained through later reflection. For now, the two couples—with the Craddocks' daughter, Chelsea, toddling in their midst—had embarked upon what was going to prove a grand adventure.

CHAPTER ELEVEN

Serendipity

Mark and Susan Torrance were married in Seattle, followed by a reception at Twin Islands Lodge, surrounded by friends new and old. *Courtesy of Mark Torrance*

The impetus behind Mark Torrance's drive and energy—which has been a factor in his business success and in his visionary push to restore and enhance Twin Islands Lodge—stems from his childhood. Some of his warmest memories are of time spent with his maternal grandparents, Ewart and Gazina

Upper. Their small dairy farm (now covered by highways in Washington State) was his boyhood haven. Mark helped milk cows, haul hay, tend the kitchen garden and feed the chickens, which perhaps explains why he keeps hens today, both in his urban garden in Seattle and on Twin Islands.

Part of Ewart and Gazina Upper's charm was their old-fashioned ways, but this couple had been at the cutting edge of change in their youth. Mark's grandmother Gazina had continued to work as a librarian after marrying, though this bucked social conventions of the time. And her wage outstripped her husband's earnings as a teacher.[177] She'd inherited a strong work ethic—and ambition—from her father, an electrical engineer who'd emigrated from Norway to Washington State during a deep recession in the early 1890s.

Mark Torrance's paternal history, by contrast, turned out to be nuanced. When Mark was in his mid-twenties, an uncle called to say he wanted to come around for coffee. "I only saw him a few times a year, so this was unusual," recalls Mark. His uncle felt it was time Mark knew that Kirby Torrance was not his biological father. Mark's mother, said this uncle, had been married before, in a short-lived relationship with a man named Bill Brown.

Mark eventually tracked down Bill Brown, but his father showed little interest in rekindling a relationship. It wasn't until recent years that Mark pieced together the details of his father's troubled past, some of which was revealed after his mother's death in photos, letters and clippings she had stowed away in a trunk.

In this trunk were things like a 1942 newspaper article with a photo of Bill Brown and Betsy Upper sitting before a formal restaurant setting. A waiter in a suit with a satin collar and a white bow tie pours chilled white wine into Upper's glass. She steadies it with one hand, her face half-turned to the task and suffused with a lingering smile. Brown watches, bemused, his slicked-back hair gleaming in the camera's flash. "A good-looking pair, what say," reads the caption. "This farewell to arms party doesn't seem to be a sad occasion. Miss Betsy Upper, attractive University of Washington student, and William Brown are about to drink a toast to the future! The young man left the next day for Africa to join the American Field Service."

---

177   US census data.

SERENDIPITY

Bill Brown had just graduated from the University of Washington, and he was poised to start his working life with voluntary World War II service. Betsy Upper clipped articles about the emergency unit he served with in Africa, assisting injured men and burying the dead. Sometimes the Allied soldiers had to leave bodies to rot in the desert sun in the haste of war. When Brown returned about a year later to recuperate from an injury, he and Betsy Upper were married. They shared deep bonds. Both came from upwardly mobile families, and both were painters and keen readers.

Brown was reposted within a year, this time to serve in Europe. When his platoon was surrounded and captured in France, he was sent to Poland as a prisoner-of-war. On being freed, Brown—now a scrawny wraith, suffering from dysentery—walked about 800 kilometres (497 miles) to Odessa, in Ukraine. His weight had dropped to under 45 kilograms (100 pounds). Like so many other returning vets, he had what was then called shellshock, and is now understood to be post-traumatic stress disorder. Brown wrote and painted his way through convalescence and, much later, published two books, one of them a long-form, Beat-era prose poem jointly produced by a left-leaning journal and San Francisco's avant-garde City Lights bookstore and publishing company.[178]

It was during her husband's difficult convalescence that Betsy (Upper) Brown gave birth to Mark, in May 1946. Their marriage was probably already in trouble. The bright fellow Betsy had fallen in love with was now a broken man who took refuge in alcohol. "Bill was not easy to be around some of the time and would vanish for weeks now and then," wrote one of Brown's sons from a later marriage. "Once a week or so he would call home during those times, sometimes only talking in French." Betsy and Bill Brown were divorced while Mark was still too young to remember, and her second husband, Kirby Torrance, stepped into the role of father.

Kirby Torrance was an engaged parent who encouraged Mark's entrepreneurial spirit. Mark was expected to participate in family chores from an early age. Mark was just 12 when Kirby helped him buy a gas-powered lawnmower on credit so the boy could start a mowing business. Mark repaid

---

178 Bill Brown, *We Are, Are We*, and *The Way to Uncle Sam's Hotel*, (San Francisco: City Lights Books, c. 1960).

CHAPTER ELEVEN

the loan that same summer. In the years that followed, though his parents didn't always fully understand the market and potential of the companies Mark formed, they helped finance his start and took pride in his successes.

Mark attended the University of Washington after high school, studying engineering, economics and communication. A career in "big business," as he later told a newspaper reporter, was not his initial goal, but a passion for Seattle's vibrant rock-music scene and an interest in electronics lead him in an unexpected direction. He started out arranging lighting and sound for musicians performing in clubs. Like others of this time, he collected music posters, and, in 1968, while still in university, he made and sold posters of collaged images. (One of them depicted then-US president Richard Nixon with butterflies coming out of his head.) Mark followed poster-making with a sideline business selling stereos and music systems to restauranteurs. This led to mixing music tapes for them in his home studio under the brand Yesco. With a growing clientele, he opened what he describes as a "funky storefront" with a huge sunflower painted on one wall. Things shifted into high gear for Yesco when Nordstrom's Brass Plum Boutique signed on as one of his first major accounts.

Up to this point, Seattle-based retailer Nordstrom had relied on Muzak, the leading purveyor of ambient music, but that company's bland elevator music was losing favour. Mark's concept was unique. He thought music should reflect consumers' tastes and set the mood in retail settings. "When people are more comfortable, they're going to spend more time in your place," he told a reporter.

There were setbacks for Yesco.[179] But, by 1984, business was so brisk the company had captured a substantial slice of the US market. This caught the attention of Muzak executives. In 1986, the Yesco team agreed to join with Muzak, with Mark Torrance as president.[180] "We want to bring Muzak out of the elevator and into the '80s," Mark told a newspaper reporter.[181] But catering to a corporate board wasn't a good fit for him. This—and the

---

179   *South Florida Sun Sentinel*, April 30, 1985, p. 44.
180   *Chicago Tribune*, September 10, 1986, p. 32; *The Gazette* (Montreal), January 8, 1987, p. 40.
181   *The Gazette* (Montreal), January 8, 1987, p. 40.

SERENDIPITY

dawning realization that Muzak LLC (as the company was now called) was doomed to fail, because it was impossible to dislodge its branding as elevator music—caused Mark to sell his shares.

A few years after leaving Muzak LLC, Mark and a group of Seattle-based entrepreneurs started a new company, PhotoDisc, making stock images available to designers, newspapers and magazines. Clients could choose from a catalogue available on compact discs, with royalties paid to the originating artists and photographers. The service soon morphed into an online compilation, which allowed PhotoDisc to reach a global market.

Throughout these years, Desolation Sound remained a favourite summer retreat for Mark and his then-wife, Wady Ballinger. His children have fond memories of sailing trips. They swam in the marine park's unusually warm waters (which can reach temperatures of 24 degrees Celsius, or 75 degrees Fahrenheit). They'd call friends on the VHF radio, arranging to raft together for shared meals of freshly caught fish and crab. The wilderness setting, combined with the social fun of hundreds of boats congregating in the sound, was a perfect fit for this gregarious family.

Meanwhile, Mark's company leapt from success to success. Mark's voice still rings with enthusiasm as he talks of the excitement of learning to embrace change and engage in creative problem-solving while starting two successful businesses—Yesco and PhotoDisc.

Mark's latest company caught the attention of its competitor, Getty Communications of England, which lacked PhotoDisc's IT strengths. In 1997, Mark and his partners met in a colleague's summer home in Desolation Sound, where they agreed to a merger, rebranding as Getty Images. And as he'd done with Yesco, Mark agreed to stay on the board. He soon found, however, that he didn't enjoy the role and gradually sold his shares. It had been a stimulating ride, and he missed his coworkers and peers—but he was ready to see what else life had to offer.[182]

During Mark's final years with PhotoDisc, he had formed a new relationship with Susan Summers, whom he'd first met decades before after a friend set them up with a coffee date. They had both been in their mid-twenties then. "[Susan's] beauty, how she moved, her deep voice, long blonde

---

182 Mark Torrance served on the Getty Images board for a few years thereafter.

hair, green eyes and caring demeanor" was hugely attractive, recalls Mark, but he was in a committed relationship, so he didn't follow through. In 1998, by which time both were unattached, they reconnected at Joe Golberg's birthday party. There was a guest list, recalls Mark, but a few people just showed up. Among the latter was Susan Summers. They went for lunch after the party, just before Susan left for travel in Nepal. When she returned, they became a couple.

Mark Torrance and Susan Summers were still in the flush of new romance when he bought south Twin in February 2000, drawing upon proceeds from the sale of his shares in Getty Images. They were married in Seattle on May 1, and later held a wedding party in Twin's lodge. The long wooden dining table, built over sixty years before by Dick and Ethel Andrews, was spread with an array of food. Susan wore a wraparound dress she'd made herself with white lace and a Japanese print fabric in golds and greens. The newlyweds repeated their vows before old friends and new in front of the lodge's baronial stone fireplace. Both had entered a new phase in their lives, with limitless possibilities for them—and for Twin Islands.

CHAPTER TWELVE

Taking Wing

The Twin Islands lodge still retains its old-world feel. *Wendy Reifel*

If the Torrances had known they'd have just fifteen years together before cancer would claim Susan's life, perhaps they would have scaled back the jam-packed schedule that followed their marriage in 2000. But they didn't. Instead, they dove headlong into their new passions. Susan took up gardening and learned to paint portraits, birds, and landscapes in oils and charcoals.

CHAPTER TWELVE

They both learned to fly seaplanes, expediting their frequent commutes between Twin Islands and Seattle.[183]

Mark established a charitable foundation, redirecting the energy he'd poured into his demanding career. Through it, he provides grants to organizations that tackle "social and environmental challenges, with new and creative approaches," says his website. He supports causes like the preservation of the Great Bear Rainforest on British Columbia's pristine central coast, the United Republic Fund (a non-partisan organization focused on eliminating corruption in US politics), and community projects on Quadra and Cortes.

What to do with Twin's massive lodge was a quandary for the Torrances. Visual artist and writer Judith Williams and her husband, Bobo Fraser, visited shortly after the Torrances bought Twin. Mark floated the idea of tearing the massive lodge down and using the materials to build a cluster of cabins. Judith was incensed—and her response brought the historical significance of the building into sharper focus for Mark. Shortly thereafter, Judith located Marian (Andrews) Harrison, whose parents had built the lodge. Marian was in her senior years and losing her eyesight, but she and her son, John, agreed to come to Twin for a visit.

Mark's son, Tom, happened to be staying, and he generally occupied what had formerly been Marian's room, but he turned it over to Marian. "The [lodge] looks exactly the way it was when my parents built it," she later told Judith Williams. The bedcovers, carpets and even the vases her mother had bought so long ago in Vancouver were still in use.

John Harrison lent Mark a family photo album to be scanned. Dozens of sepia-toned black-and-white images, shot both on land and from the air, documented the building of the lodge and the years shortly thereafter.

Marian Harrison's visit cemented the Torrances's resolve to restore the lodge, and they both took an active role. "[Susan] embraced the island completely," remembers caretaker Sonia Craddock. "Every corner of it. And the [lodge] wasn't entirely loveable at first—with its musty, mouse-infested buildings—but she was a positive person."

---

183   Mark Torrance published a book on this airline, under his imprint Earmark: C. Marin Faure, *Success on the Step: Flying with Kenmore Air*, (Seattle: Earmark, 2004).

The two women, though about a decade apart in age, bonded deeply, working side by side to expand and plant the garden. Sonia was struck by Susan's charisma and her quiet grace, and she admired her new friend's vivacity and confidence. "She drew people and action into her orbit," concurred a later caretaker.[184]

Mark and Jay likewise developed close bonds as they hashed out ideas for the restoration of the lodge and its infrastructure. Jay appreciated Mark's willingness to weigh and incorporate input from others. "We'd talk things over once or twice, then he'd go away and think about it," recalls Jay. "We'd talk it over again and things would gel." Mark grew restless at such times, doing other tasks before returning to the discussion with fresh thoughts. "When he gets on a track, he's unstoppable," says Jay. "He creates a kind of bubble of activity, and everything in it is self-circulating and sustaining." Mark, in turn, marvelled at the younger man's almost intuitive connection to the land and sea. "He can smell when salmon are around," says Mark. Jay also proved to have an uncanny ability to navigate in any weather, always getting the Torrances to a dock on Cortes or the Malaspina Peninsula on time for a return flight to Seattle.

There was no cellphone coverage or internet connection on Twin when the Torrances bought the place. Though the lodge had been a marvel for its state-of-the-art radiophone during the World War II era, there was now just a patched-together telephone service via a neighbouring home on Cortes. The Torrances installed a microwave dish outside the lodge's master bedroom, attempting to pick up a signal from Mount Washington on Vancouver Island, but it proved weak. "If you jiggled the floorboards the wrong way the connection was lost," recalls Mark. The solution was to install an internet repeater on north Twin's peak, which provided a strong signal.

Twin's crew expanded with the growing complexity of the restoration project. Engineer Dennis Hansen of Cortes masterminded many of the structural details, and he mentored Jay Craddock and his crew.

Jay had just basic carpentry skills when he started work for the Torrances, but he was a quick study. He was eager to try new things and had a nimble capacity to learn. In this, he had much in common with Charlie

---

184 Fiona Reid, telephone interview.

CHAPTER TWELVE

Rasmussen, the lodge's construction foreman of six decades earlier. Looking back now, Jay says his ten years on Twin were the experience of a lifetime. "I got paid to learn—and the schooling I got was amazing."

The lodge needed work from top to bottom. Dennis Hansen repointed the beach-stone foundations (relining the joins with fresh grout) and rebuilt the fireplace. Susan Torrance was a passionate cook, so they upgraded the small, old-fashioned kitchen. Jay cut interior walls open to incorporate storerooms and a stairway to the basement to create a much larger kitchen, with a half-wall opening into the dining room. He also cut openings in the exterior walls of these rooms for French doors leading onto a new deck, which became the lodge's main entrances. "That was one of the hardest things I did," says Jay, remembering the first chainsaw cut. "It felt like a travesty because the building was in such original condition."

The outbuildings were in even more urgent need of repairs. The crew rebuilt the farmhouse—or Pete's Cabin, as it's now called[185]—which was on the verge of collapse. The Torrances had five wells drilled and a new boat dock installed. They expanded and refurbished the caretaker's house and built new decks on the lodge, using a portable sawmill to cut lumber from waste logs that Jenks and Shields' logging crew had left behind. They also cut lumber for a 929-square-metre (10,000-square-foot) barn with a suite for part-time staff.

"We had free creative licence," recalls Sonia Craddock.

"Yeah, I got to play like I was a millionaire," added Jay, who says it felt like anything was possible. "It was pretty frigging cool."

In 2004, the Torrances bought north Twin from Endswell. They left it largely undisturbed, using it mainly as the site for a long bank of solar panels on its south-facing shore, and the internet repeater on its highest peak.

The Torrances visited Twin at least once a month in winter and lived there almost full-time from early summer through fall. Everyone worked hard. "Ten years went by in a flash," recalls Jay. "You could hardly stop for tea, there was so much work to do. There were crews around nonstop."

---

185 No one currently knows the source of this name, but it may have been applied in memory of caretaker Pete Banning, who lived in this house from 1939 to 1956.

But when the Craddocks' daughter, Chelsea, reached her teens, it was time to move to Quadra Island, where there was easier access to schools. Jay and Sonia were feeling exhausted by this time. They were ready to devote time to their own pursuits, but they missed Twin and the Torrances, who'd become like family. "The problem with us was we could do everything—so we did," recalls Jay. "It took me at least four years to not think about [Twin] anymore."

After the Craddocks left, work on Twin slowed somewhat, but alternative energy projects continued to be implemented.

"Has he talked to you about batteries yet?" Mark Torrance's daughter, Allie Okner, asked me in a 2019 telephone interview. Onsite-generated energy and storage systems have long been her father's passion.

It was this interest in alternative energy and environmentalism that attracted Twin's next caretakers in 2008.[186] Delia Becker and Scott Rempel had lived in remote coastal locales for over thirty years when they met the Torrances, who had made a donation to a salmon enhancement project Delia and Scott were working on. The new caretakers accepted the job on Twin with the understanding it would evolve into a part-time commitment, allowing them to continue to do habitat restoration work. They had extra help, and the Torrances slowed the pace of new developments, but the caretaking job continued to be all-consuming.

During Delia and Scott's nearly four years on Twin, they focused on reducing energy consumption in the caretaker's house. This goal turned into a friendly rivalry, as each household pushed to reduce and reuse. But one of Delia and Scott's proudest achievements was the building of a large greenhouse in the garden.

Wolves were prevalent on south Twin during their tenure, resulting in a decreased deer population, which meant there were many acres of grass to mow. To help with this, they bought a 317.5-kilogram (700-pound) heifer, "Rocket the Cow," to butcher at season's end. Rocket kept the grass in check, and her bulky presence proved a deterrent to the wolves, but when it came time for slaughter, no one could face the deed. The cow wound up going to pasture on Cortes.

---

186   The Twin Islands accounting records show Delia Becker and Scott Rempel worked on Twin from September 2008 to May 2011.

CHAPTER TWELVE

In the interval, the deer population rose again, and without Rocket's intimidating presence, the wolves returned. "One day I got out of the shower and there was a wolf running by at high speed, tearing through the compound," recalls Scott. When he shot over the wolf's head to scare it off, someone working in the garden became concerned for Twin's wolves. The proposed solution was the purchase of Irish wolfhounds, hearkening back to the Andrews family's era on Twin, but even these dogs would prove unequal to the task. One of them was attacked and seriously injured in a face-off with the wolves.

Scottish immigrants Fiona and Douglas Reid replaced Delia Becker and Scott Rempel in May 2011. They had worked in a fishing lodge on the west coast for a time, followed by a year as caretakers on Hernando. They were living in Ontario when they saw the posting for a couple to serve as caretakers on Twin. Douglas missed the sea—he had been a marine biologist and a commercial fisherman in his youth—so they applied for the job. They piled their things into their truck and a travel trailer and headed west for an interview with the Torrances. Halfway across the country, they questioned the wisdom of this long trip, with nothing more than the Torrances' assurance they were lead candidates. They called from somewhere on the Prairies and Susan urged them on. When they arrived in Seattle, Mark invited them to bring their dog in for the interview, and though it barked throughout and snapped at Mark when he tried to calm it, the Reids got the job. Fiona's enthusiasm for gardening, and Douglas's boating skills and jack-of-all-trades background, made them a good fit.

The Reids hadn't been on the job long before Susan began to suffer debilitating headaches. She sometimes fell silent and disappeared from the dinner table without a word. In photographs from this time, Mark recognizes the pain etched on Susan's face. Tests revealed she had an aggressive form of brain cancer called glioblastoma, which was largely untreatable.

"Can you believe that I've got brain cancer and that I'm dying?" she said to Mark one day, as they walked one of Twin's trails.[187] Just the year before, when life seemed to stretch far into the future, she'd made plans to take up painting in acrylics. She and Mark also wanted to travel, now that work on

---

[187] Telephone interview with Mark Torrance's friend Joe Golberg.

Twin was easing. But on August 26, 2012, Susan died in Mark's arms at a hospital in Seattle, at the age of 64. She was surrounded by friends, family and flowers from her urban garden.

When I asked what Mark would have changed, had he known their time together would be so short, his thoughts darted back to their first meeting. "I would have called her back after that first coffee date," he said. "Just before Susan died, she told me the maddest she had ever been with me was when I did not contact her after that blind date."

Susan's death left a yawning gap in Mark's life and it was over five years before he finally regained interest in Twin. "It's time to carry on now," he said in 2018, "and continue the work of creating a legacy on these islands."

Today, Mark spends holidays on Twin Islands and draws huge pleasure from its forests and meadows, heritage buildings, kitchen garden and orchards. In a time of deep global unrest and a lack of concrete action by those in power to mitigate catastrophic environmental change, he looks to Twin as a self-sufficient haven. It will be his refuge, should predictions of a dystopian future come to pass.

On a more optimistic note, Twin serves as a model for renewable systems. "Today on Twin," writes Mark, "our creature comforts are supplied by solar and hydro power harnessed from the earth and sun, and we draw our inner power from immersion in the natural world." What lies ahead for Twin is an unknown, but the protective covenants and meticulous restoration work of its buildings and services will ensure these jewel-like islands and their heritage structures will remain largely intact, while the ever-changing world spins on.

Acknowledgements

Getting to know Twin Islanders—current and former owners, caretakers and staff—was a huge privilege. John Harrison and his cousin Wendy Andrews shared their archival records and research into Dick and Ethel Andrews's World War II-era lives. Rita Rasmussen and Adrian (North) Redford, whose parents played lead roles in the building of Twin Islands Lodge, provided memories and photographs. Special thanks to Rita for her attention to detail and assistance with manuscript drafts.

Dozens of others have likewise given time and skill. George Reifel, who has a seasonal home on neighbouring Hernando Island, was always at the ready with sage advice, insights and records. He introduced me to people like Mike Jenks, owner of the islands in 1997–8, and Rob Straight, whose father was part-owner of Twin in the late 1950s and 1960s.

Cortes Islanders Carol Newell, Joel Solomon, Iris Steigmann, Ginnie Ellingsen, Judith Williams, Bobo Fraser and Doreen (Calwell) Guthrie opened their homes and memories.

Adrian (North) Redford and Rita Rasmussen. *Jeanette Taylor*

ACKNOWLEDGEMENTS

Prince Bernhard of Baden, in Germany, had heartfelt recollections of summers on Twin. And his family's various caretakers—Julie Neal, Shirley Whitehouse (formerly Lott) and Paul and Magdalene Knepperges—contributed photos and recollections.

Caretakers from the Torrance's years—including Jay and Sonia Craddock, Scott Rempel and Delia Becker, and Doug and Fiona Reid—were generous with their time. (Special thanks go to the Craddocks, who served me cookies and tea over several long visits.)

Fellow history buff Jon Ackroyd was a huge help with initial research. I'm indebted to my writers' group for their insightful questions: Julie Douglas, Dionne LaPoint-Bakota, Carol Gall, Libby King, Michael Redican and Ralph Keller. Michael Redican and Elise Cote edited the original manuscript for a book which Mark Torrance produced as a gift he gave to everyone who attended a celebratory party on Twin in 2019. Like Harbour Publishing's editor for this edition, Ariel Brewster, they were insightful and patient. It was enlightening to work will all three of them.

The staff of both the Cortes Island Museum and the Museum at Campbell River provided enthusiastic assistance. The Powell River Museum's digitized newspaper records were valuable. I also sourced information at the BC Archives, BC Lands Branch in Victoria, the University of British Columbia's Special Collections, the Glenbow Museum, the University of Victoria's Special Collections and the Vancouver Island Regional Library.

Drew Blaney of the Tla'amin Nation was supportive, as was ethnographer/linguist Randy Bouchard. Retired head of the BC Archaeological Sites Branch, Steve Acheson, interpreted archaeological records; and Jeff Beddoes, former head of the BC Lands Branch, helped with survey records. David Caulfield shed light on Twin's geology.

Mark Torrance's friends and family were generous with their time. Special thanks go to Mark's executive assistant, Karin Cirillo, and to Molly Bullard of Seattle Photo Organizing, for their fully engaged support. (Molly's photo work and design for Mark Torrance's edition of the book made it an attractive gift for Twin Islanders!) Mark's long-time friend Joe Golberg shared honest and thoughtful reflections. And last, but not least, Mark Torrance was a delight to work with, providing open, responsive, honest and energized input throughout.

As always, Gerry Cote, my life partner, was my sounding board, first reader and kayaking companion for explorations of Twin.

Index

Pages in **bold** indicate a photo.

Abelson, Martha, 126
Anderson, Bernie, 116–17, 126
Andrews family
  Andrews, Bill, 49–**50**–52, 96
  Andrews, Dick (Richard Magill), 10, **45**, 48–**50**, **59**, **68**, 74, **86**
    adolescence, 44, 46
    decease, 96
    in Japan, 51–52, 54–58, 60, 85, 94
    in Korea, 50–51
    in Vancouver, 83–87, 93
    on Twin Islands, 62–65
  Andrews, Dick Junior, 49
  Andrews, Elizabeth Ann, 51–52
  Andrews (Hosking), Ethel, **9**–10, 47, **50**, **59**, **68**, **86**, **93**
    early life, 46
    in Japan, 52
    in Korea, 50–51
    decease, 96
    on Twin, 76, 93
    wedding trousseau, 48
  Andrews (Harrison), Marian, **9**, 52, 54, 60, **88**, 94–95, 117
  Andrews, Wendy, 49

Wong, Tonie, **9**, 52–**53**, 57–58, 85, 87, 94
Andrews & George, import business, 44, 48–49, 51–52, 56, 58
Anne, Princess, **110**, 114
Banning, Pete, 89, 91–92, 96, 98
Becker, Delia, 149–50
Bell, Max, 98, 103, 107–9
Berton, Pierre, 103
Brown, Bill, 140–41
Canoe Passage, 18
Castillou, Harry, 99
Craddock, Jay, 125, 132–33, 135–38
Craddock, Sonia, 132–33, 135–38
Cortes Island, 31
  Mansons Landing, 17, 25
  population of, 14
Daido Shoji K.K., 85
D'Angio, John, 66, 71, 77
Dowling, Veronica, 106–7
Elizabeth II, Queen, **110**, 112, 114, **118**–**119**–**120**–121
Ellingsen, Ginnie, 118–19
Endswell, 128, 133, 135–37, 148
European first contact, 22–24
Fanning, Oscar and Hilda, 106–7
"Flea Village", 24
Fraser, Bobo, 123, 134–35, 146
geography, of Twin, 13–14
geology, of Twin, 15–16
Gmeiner, Lella, 116–17
Grafin Theresia of Abensberg and Traun, 111
Harrison, John, 11, 48–49, 85, 94
Harrison, Slim, 94
Hollyhock Leadership Learning

INDEX

Centre, 127–28
Indigenous stewardship, of Twin, 17–22, 25
Jenks, Mike, 123–30
Johann of Thun and Hohenstein, Count, 111
Jones, William, 32
Karuizawa Lodge, 54–55
Keenleyside, Dr. Hugh, 58
Knepperges, Magdalene, 117–18, 122–25
Knepperges, Paul, 117–**19**, 122–25
Lacey, Bob, 116
Langdon, Bob, 101, 112–13
Lodge, Twin Islands, 62, **78–79**, **81**
   caretaker's cabin, **69**
   cost to build, 73
   construction of, 63–**73–74–75**, 77
   furnishing of, 76–77
   infrastructure, 11, 74–77, 147–49
   landscaping for, 80
   sale of, 94–96, 100, 111, 122
   shellfish lease, 80
   Twin Islands Lodge Ltd., 98, 105
Lott, George, 106, 108, 111
Lott (Whitehouse), Shirley, 107, 109, 112–13
Mackinnon, John Maclellan, 35–36
Magill Export Import Ltd, 87
Manson, Anna, Jack, and Nicol, **33**
Manson, John and Margaret, 30, 37
Maquinna Investments, 84
McCauley, Clara and Joseph, 40, 42–43
McGee, "Old" George, 25–**26**
McDonald, Donald (Dan), 28–32
McKay (Manson), Rose, 30, 34, **41**
McMahon, Diane, 103–4
Mounce, Bill, **104**–5, 107–8
Mounce, Helen, **104**–5
Nash, Dick, 43
Nash (McCauley), Dorothy, **41**–43
Neal, Del and Julie, 114, 117
Newell, Carol, 128–**29**–31, 133
Nixon, James, 32–**33**–**34**, 36, 39–40
Nixon, Margaret, **28**, 32–**33**–**34**–36, 39, 40
Nixon, Reverend Harpur Colville, 32–**33**, 35–38
North, Alex, 67–**68**, 77, 80, 91
North (Redford), Adrian, 67–68, **91**–**92**, **152**
North, Aino, 68, 71, **91**
Okner, Allie, 149
Parker, Len, 77, 80, 115
Paulley, Kim, 120
Pearson, Lester B., 107–**8**
Philip, Prince, **110**, 112–14, 118
Rasmussen, Charlie, **9**, 63–**64**–**67**–**68**–69, 71, 73, 76–77, 80, 89–90, 114
Rasmussen (Goski), Helge, **9**, 69–**70**–**72**, 77, 89–90, 114
Rasmussen, Rita, 10–11, 80, 91, 114–15, **152**
Reid, Douglas and Fiona, 150
Reifel, George, 124, 128–30, 133, 135, 137
Rempel, Scott, 149–50
Roethel, Henry, 109, 111, 117
Shields, Peter, 124, 129
Sirk, George, 120

INDEX

Solomon, Joel, 127–30, 133, 137
Spilsbury, Jim, 65, 77, 85, 87
Steigemann, Iris, 126
Straight, Hal, **97**–103, 105–6, 109
Straight, Rob, **97**–**98**–99, 102
Summers, Susan, 134–**39**, 144–51
Sutton, Thomas, 39
Tl'umnachm, 17
Torrance, Kirby, 140–41
Torrance, Mark, **139**
  career, 142–44
  childhood, 139–42
  purchase of Twin Islands, 134–51
  Twin Islands legacy, 145–51
Twin Islands, **13**
Twin Isles, **83**
Union Steamship Company, 31, 100–101
"Ulloa", 24, 105
Upper, Betsy, 140–41
Upper, Ewart and Gazina, 140
von Baden family
  Bernhard, Prince, 111–12, 114–15
  Berthold, Margrave, 111–13
  Leopold, Prince, 114, **119**
  Marie-Louise, Princess, 114
  Maximilian, Margrave, 111, 113–**19**
  Michael, Prince, 114, 119
  Theodora, Margravine, 111–13
  Valerie, Margravine, 113
Walker, Cliff, 105–6, 109
Weaver, Bill, 120
Webster, Jack, 102
Williams, Judith, 123
Wong, Tonie. *See under* Andrews family

Bibliography

Angelbeck, William O. *They Recognize No Superior Chief, Power, Practice, Anarchism and Warfare in the Coast Salish Past.* PhD thesis, Vancouver: University of British Columbia, 2009.

Barnett, Homer. *The Coast Salish of British Columbia.* Eugene: University of Oregon, 1995.

Fedje, Daryl, Duncan McLaren, Thomas S. James, Quentin Mackie, Nicole F. Smith, John R. Southon, and Alexander P. Mackie. "A revised sea level history for the north Strait of Georgia, British Columbia, Canada." *Quaternary Science Reviews* 192 (July 15, 2018): 300–316. doi.org/10.1016/j.quascirev.2018.05.018.

Johnson, Sarah Elizabeth. *Tla'amin Cultural Landscape: Combining traditional knowledge with archaeological investigation in Grace Harbour, Desolation Sound, BC.* MA thesis, Burnaby, BC: Simon Fraser University, 2010.

Keenleyside, Hugh L. *Hammer the Golden Days.* Vol. 1, *Memoirs of Hugh L. Keenleyside.* Toronto, ON: McClelland and Stewart, 1981.

Kennedy, Dorothy, and Randy Bouchard. *Sliammon Life, Sliammon Lands.* Vancouver, BC: Talonbooks, 1983.

McFarlane, Gordon, and Richard Beamish. *The Sea Among Us, The Amazing Strait of Georgia.* Madeira Park: Harbour Publishing, 2014.

Parsley, Colleen. *Archaeological Impact Assessment of DjSc-1, Shelter Point Project*. Nanaimo: Aquilla Archaeology, 2013.

Patrick, Lyana Marie. *Storytelling in the Fourth World: Exploration of Meaning of Place and Tla'amin Resistance to Dispossession*. MA thesis, Victoria, BC: University of Victoria, 1997.

Suttles, Wayne, ed. *The Handbook of North American Indians*. Washington, DC: Smithsonian Institution, 1990.

Thompson, Bill. *Once Upon a Stump, Times and Tales of Powell River Pioneer*. Powell River, BC: Powell River Heritage Research Association, 1993.

White, Howard, and Jim Spilsbury. *Spilsbury's Coast, Pioneer Years in the Wet West*. Madeira Park: Harbour Publishing, 1987.

About the Author

Jeanette Taylor started her career in history transcribing taped interviews in the British Columbia Archives, followed by twenty years on the Campbell River Museum's curatorial staff, and latterly as the executive director of the Campbell River Art Gallery.

Jeanette has five coastal history books in print, including *The Quadra Story: A History of Quadra Island* and *Tidal Passages: A History of the Discovery Islands*. She leads multi-day heritage sites cruises aboard the historic *Columbia III*; and assists nonfiction writers through classes and manuscript reviews.

Jeanette works in the office of her 1894 log farmhouse on Quadra Island, overlooking gardens, orchards and the sea.